THREE HARVESTS

and the

DRAGNET

The Trumpet Call

SANCTUS MATTHEWS

Thy kingdom come, Thy will be done, on earth as it is in heaven. Afterwards He sat down at the right hand of His Father...and then the King will say to those on His right hand-the place of authority and honor- "Come, blessed of my Father, inherit the kingdom prepared for you from the foundation of the world." And to the goats on His left hand He will say "You have inherited a place of dishonor-for your works are burned up not having passed the test of the fire and hammer of the living Word of God. For Abraham's descendants were promised an inheritance of the gates of their enemies, the gates of governance and judgment, to be a blessing to the nations through the foundation and faith found in the Messiah. For many will come from the east and the west to sit down with the living testimony of Abraham, Isaac and Jacob, with all of those who have called upon Jesus Christ as Savior." For as some poets have said, "For in Him we live and move and exist." So, we will hear the clarion call. With a mysterious song the wicked will not understand it will be sung. The secrets will unveil a season of new birth: a season to rebuild. Go forth in tears bearing precious seed. For now begins the season of harvest for the righteous and for the wicked.

THREE HARVESTS
and their
RIDDLES FROM BEGINNING TO END

WHEN TWO PEOPLE WILL BE STANDING IN A FIELD, SUDDENLY ONE WILL BE TAKEN AWAY BY THE LORD'S SERVANTS FOR JUDGMENT BY THE FIRE AND SWORD OF THE WORD (ISAIAH 2:4; MATTHEW 13:40; 24:40; JEREMIAH 5:14; 23:29; HEBREWS 4:12; EPHESIANS 6:17; REVELATION 2:18 AMPLIFIED).

"THE THIEF COMES ONLY IN ORDER TO STEAL AND KILL AND DESTROY. I CAME THAT THEY MAY HAVE AND ENJOY LIFE, AND HAVE IT IN ABUNDANCE [TO THE FULL, TILL IT OVERFLOWS]" (JOHN 10:10 AMP).

HARVEST OF THRONES OF JUDGMENT
FOR THE RIGHTEOUS

GENESIS 22:17-18
DANIEL 7:18
MATTHEW 13:43
1 CORINTHIANS 6:2
REVELATION 20:4

HARVEST OF SOULS OF THOSE WHO BELIEVE

PROVERBS 11:30
DANIEL 12:3
MATTHEW 13:47-50
REVELATION 14:14-16

HARVEST OF JUDGEMENT
FOR THE WICKED WHO OPPOSE THE TRUTH

PSALM 64:7-8
PSALM 149:6-9
PROVERBS 24:23
MATTHEW 13:47-50
JUDE 1:14-16
REVELATION 11
REVELATION 19:20

THE TRIBULATION CUT SHORT

*"And if those days [of tribulation] had not been cut short,
no human life would be saved; but for the sake of the elect
[God's chosen ones] those days will be shortened"
(Matthew 24:22 AMP)*

FORETOLD FROM THE BEGINNING

*Great distress foretold in the song of Moses
(Deuteronomy 31:29; Revelation 15:3).*

♫ **Pause and listen to *End of the Age: Book One, "The Song of Moses."*** ♫

*"Who has performed and done this, calling forth [and
guiding the destinies of] the generations [of the nations]
from the beginning? I, the LORD—the first, and with
the last [existing before history began, the ever-present, un-
changing God]—I am He.'"
(Isaiah 41:4 AMP).*

*"Declaring the end and the result **from the beginning**,
And from ancient times the things which have not [yet] been
done, Saying, 'My purpose will be established, And I will do
all that pleases Me and fulfills My purpose'"
(Isaiah 46:10 AMP).*

FROM THE BEGINNING?
CHAPTER AND VERSE, TRACED THROUGH THE WORD.

*"He made known to us the mystery of His will according
to His good pleasure, which He purposed in Christ, **with
regard to the fulfillment of the times [that is, the
end of history, the climax of the ages]—to bring
all things together in Christ, [both] things in the
heavens and things on the earth.** In him also we have
received an inheritance [a destiny—we were claimed by
God as His own], having been predestined (chosen, appointed beforehand) according to the purpose of Him who works*

everything in agreement with the counsel and design of His
will, so that we who were the first to hope in Christ [who first
put our confidence in Him as our Lord and Savior] would
exist to the praise of His glory"
(Ephesians 1:9-12 AMP).

HARVEST OF THRONES FOR THE RIGHTEOUS

"Indeed I will greatly bless you, and I will greatly multiply
your seed like the stars of the heavens and like the sand
on the seashore; and your seed shall possess the gate of their
enemies [as conquerors].Through your seed all the nations of
the earth shall be blessed, because you have heard and obeyed
My voice."
(Genesis 22:17-18 AMP). — From the Beginning

THE "THRONES" ARE SET UP "IN THE GATE." THIS WAS THE
SEAT OF GOVERNANCE IN DAYS OF OLD. (DEUTERONOMY
16:18)

"But the saints (believers) of the Most High [God] will re-
ceive the kingdom and possess the kingdom forever, for all
ages to come."
(Daniel 7:18 AMP).

"Then THE RIGHTEOUS [those who seek the will of God]
WILL SHINE FORTH [radiating the new life] LIKE
THE SUN in the kingdom of their Father. He who has ears
[to hear], let him hear and heed My words."
(Matthew 13:43 AMP).

"Do you not know that the saints (God's people) will [one
day] judge and govern the world? And if the world [itself]
is to be judged by you, are you unworthy and incompetent to
try [such petty matters] of the smallest courts of justice?"
(1 Corinthians 6:2 AMP).

*"And then I saw **thrones**, and sitting on them were those to*
whom judgment [that is, the authority to act as judges] was
given. And I saw the souls of those who had been beheaded

*because of their testimony of Jesus and because of the word of God, and those who had refused to worship the beast or his image, and had not accepted his mark on their forehead and on their hand; and they came to life and **reigned** with Christ for a thousand years."*
(Revelation 20:4 AMP).—AT THE END

HARVEST OF SOULS WHO BELIEVE

"Those who are [spiritually] wise will shine brightly like the brightness of the expanse of heaven, and those who lead many to righteousness, [will shine] like the stars forever and ever."
(Daniel 12:3 AMP).

"Again, the kingdom of heaven is like a dragnet which was lowered into the sea, and gathered fish of every kind, and when it was full, they dragged it up on the beach; and they sat down and sorted out the good fish into baskets, but the worthless ones they threw away."
(Matthew 13:47-48A AMP).

"Again I looked, and this is what I saw: a white cloud, and sitting on the cloud was One like the Son of Man, with a crown of gold on His head and a sharp sickle [of swift judgment] in His hand. And another angel came out of the temple, calling with a loud voice to Him who was sitting upon the cloud, "Put in Your sickle and reap [at once], for the hour to reap [in judgment] has arrived, because the earth's harvest is fully ripened. So He who was sitting on the cloud cast His sickle over the earth, and the earth was reaped (judged)."
(Revelation 14:14-16 AMP).

SITTING ON A WHITE CLOUD OF SAINTS, A CLOUD OF WIT-NESSES.

HARVEST OF JUDGEMENT
FOR THE WICKED WHO OPPOSE THE TRUTH

*"Hide me from the secret counsel and conspiracy of the ungodly, From the scheming of those who do wrong. **But God will shoot them with an [unexpected] arrow; Suddenly they will be wounded. So they will be caused to stumble. Their own tongue is against them; All who gaze at them will shake the head [in scorn].***"*
(Psalm 64:2, 7-8 AMP).

*"Put in the sickle [of judgment], for the harvest is ripe; Come, tread [the grapes], for the wine press is full; The vats overflow, for the wickedness [of the people] is great. Multitudes, multitudes in the valley of decision (judgment)! For the day of the Lord is near in the valley of decision [**when judgment is executed**].*"
(Joel 3:13-14 AMP).

*"Let the high praises of God be in their throats, And a two-edged sword in their hands, To execute vengeance on the nations And punishment on the peoples, To bind their kings with chains And their nobles with fetters of iron, **To execute on them the judgment written.** This is the honor for all His godly ones. Praise the Lord! (Hallelujah!)*"
(Psalm 149:6-9 AMP).

"...and the enemy who sowed them is the devil, and the harvest is **the end of the age**; and the reapers are angels. *"
(Matthew 13:39 AMP).

*"...but the worthless ones they threw away. So it will be at the end of the age; **the angels will come and separate the wicked from the righteous** and throw the wicked into the furnace of fire; in that place there will be weeping [over sorrow and pain] and grinding of teeth over distress and anger.*"
(Matthew 13:47-51 AMP).

*"..it was about these people that Enoch, in the seventh gen-eration from Adam, prophesied, when he said, "**Look, the Lord came with myriads of His holy ones to execute judgement upon all, and to convict all the ungodly of all the ungodly deeds they have done in an ungod-ly way and of all the harsh and cruel things ungodly way and of all the harsh and cruel things ungodly sinners have spoken against Him.** These people are [ha-bitual] murmurers, gripping and complaining, following after their own desires [controlled by passion]; they speak arrogantly, flattering people to gain an advantage.*
(Jude 1:14-16 AMP)

Rebuke the nations that delight in war! Rebuke the wicked with the sword and fire of God's written word which is established in heaven forever!

*"All Scripture is God-breathed [given by divine inspira-tion] and is profitable for **instruction**, for **conviction** [of sin], for **correction** [of error and **restoration** to **obedi-ence**], for training in righteousness [learning to live in con-formity to God's will, both publicly and privately-behaving honorably with personal integrity and moral courage]"*
(2 Timothy 3:16 AMP).

"As for you, the anointing [the special gift, the preparation] which you received from Him remains [permanently] in you, and you have no need for anyone to teach you. But just as His anointing teaches you [giving you insight through the presence of the Holy Spirit] about all things, and is true and is not a lie, and just as His anointing has taught you, you must remain in Him [being rooted in Him, knit to Him]"
(1 John 2:27 AMP).

"Do not love the world [of sin that opposes God and His precepts], nor the things that are in the world. If anyone loves the world, the love of the Father is not in him. For all that is in the world—the lust and sensual craving of the

*flesh and the lust and longing of the eyes and the boastful
pride of life [pretentious confidence in one's resources or in
the stability of earthly things]—these do not come from the
Father, but are from the world"
(1 John 2:15-16 AMP).*

For my father, who entered the fiery flame in an attempt to save his comrades only to be forcibly removed by those who arrived on the scene. Your survival, a miracle of God, is why I am here today.

Contents

Voice VII: Songs in the Night

Preface

It is all connected

The whisper of hope and promise of "Thy kingdom come, thy will be done, on earth as it is in heaven" (Matthew 6:10) came to Abraham and his descendants in the faith beginning in Genesis 22:17. It was repeated in the Psalms of David and prophesied by Daniel, the New Testament as well as in Revelation (Psalm 2; 22-23; 45; 72; 89; 110; Daniel 7:22, Revelation 20:4). Jesus referred to it as a time of the harvest of this promise, of which He is the foundation, occurring at the end of the age (John 3:16-19; 1 Corinthians 3:10-12; Matthew 13:39, Matthew 8:11), a time when renewal in the earth would begin (Matthew 19:28). This is the time when the sword of division between belief and unbelief is wielded in its full strength in the earth (Matthew 10:34 AMP).

God has always sought to bring peace to man and satisfy his spiritual thirst (John 4; 7:38; 14:27). In Christianity God seeks man. In other religions man seeks a way to their god.

God has made a way and provided an entry door to life already (John 14:6; Revelation 3:20). He has a name. Unfaithful foolish men have, on the other hand, sought to quarrel (Proverbs 20:3) and control one another instead of serving one another in love (Matthew 22:37-39). So, the hope was buried in the ground with the testimony of the martyrs and hidden in the ancient texts. Centuries pass until the key of David opens the hidden treasure of the Kingdom of Heaven in Jesus Christ (Isaiah 29:11; Proverbs 25:2; Isaiah 22:22; Matthew 13:44; Revelation 3:7). But still there are those who refuse to even listen and believe in faith (Hebrews 11:6; Jude 1:12-16). They look for justification of every vice known to God and man. For "there is no God. God will not require anything of me" (Psalm 10:4; 14:1; 36:1; 53:1). Yes, there is judgment after death (Hebrews 9:27); but this is the season of inheritance for the just and the unjust. For the meek inherit the earth (Isaiah 65:8-10; Matthew 5:5) in unity (John 17:23 AMP) and in the bond of peace (Ephesians 2:14; 2 Timothy 2:24).

Still, saints will fight the wicked with the Word of Truth in due time (Ecclesiastes 3:8; Ephesians 6:10-18; Hebrews 4:12-13; Revelation 12:11; 19:13-15). At this time the saints are quickened with strength to reign, as was promised. To govern. In the city gate. In the gates of their enemies. To be a blessing with righteous judgment (Genesis 22:17; Deuteronomy 16:18; Proverbs 24:25 AMP; 1 John 3:10 AMP). In Christ.

Selah.

Wash your garments. Listen for the Trumpet. Meanwhile, sow the seed wherever you go. Let the weeds grow along with the good grain until the time. At this time, we cut down the weeds and bundle them for the fire (Jeremiah 23:29). Then gather the wheat into the barn (Matthew 13:30).

Visions and Dreams (Joel 2:28 "...and your young men will see visions.")

Sometime in the spring of 1998 I was in a worship service. Eyes closed. Hands reaching forward at hip height. Sensing the presence of God's Spirit during the music. In a moment I had a vision of the earth suspended in the space between my hands. As it hovered there my hands felt heavy. In my spirit I could see my hands swell up, feeling suddenly warm, and surrounding the earth. The next moment the vision was gone. Fast forward to today. It is October, 2025. I remember the vision and write it here for you, the reader, because I am supposed to share it with you. After you read this book, you will share your own story as I share mine with you. "For they overcame by the blood of the Lamb and the word of their testimony" (Revelation 12:11). I only share a trumpet with you. I am not He, nor do I claim to be. I only share what has been given to me by the Spirit. You, the Body of Christ, form His hands that reach around the world. Gather the workers and reach with me (Matthew 24:30-32).

A Dream

On the evening of May 28th, 2025, I went to bed exhausted from a successful guided family fishing trip for Spoonbill that morning and cooking all afternoon. I dreamed that I had a rifle in my hands and was shooting carefully at the "enemy" on the other side of the river. I accurately picked them off with the exception of one which was dressed in white. That enemy I wounded in the head. He motioned to me to put down my rifle and engage him in combat face to face. I went into the house and retrieved my father's Naval saber. I then exited the house and walked down the bank to the edge of the river to meet him. As I approached the water's edge, the depth of the water quickly rose and I found myself floating and afraid of drowning. The dream was so intense that I could feel the water engulfing my entire body except my face so that I was just able to breathe. Abruptly waking, I lay in bed praying and received the following inspiration in my heart: the words of prophecy are the bullets that remove the enemies of confusion and doubt, for God is not the author of confusion. The enemy in white is the one who masquerades as an angel of light and is the enemy of our souls. The saber is the word of God, the Sword of the Spirit which is the word of God of Ephesians 6, for obedience and close combat, for speaking face to face and dealing with principalities and powers. The sudden rise of the river is the glory of God and river of life, the promise that God's word will cover the earth as the water covers the sea. This dream, as I understood it, represented the promise of renewal for the world and Israel after wars, shaking and much tribulation. Consider Isaiah 11:9 and Habakkuk 2:14. For man must ultimately conclude that he cannot rule himself on his own. For it is written, "Where there is no vision [no revelation of God and His word], the people are unrestrained; But happy and blessed is he who keeps the law [of God]" (Proverbs 29:18 AMP). The ground is level for all men at the foot of the cross, no matter their station in life.

This book is not about the second coming of Christ. We were told that we don't know when it would occur (Matthew 24:35-37).

In studying this book with Bible in hand, what is presented is important along with what is not presented. You need to pray for understanding.

In addition, I am not a seasoned writer. I meander back and forth through the scriptures, beginning in Genesis, to make what I have learned known to you regarding the inheritance of the promised kingdom in the earth.

There are many books out there on the end times, many of which tried to predict the second coming—they were wrong of course. So, where do we direct our questions? The apostle Paul said that the Scriptures are not of private interpretation. I agree. So is this my private interpretation? I will let you decide after you read how much scripture is used to interpret other scripture in this book, beginning with Numbers 12:6-8 where God tells Moses how he speaks to prophets. Jesus spoke in parables to veil His teaching so that those on the outside would not understand. In Revelation we read that the mystery hidden for the saints is revealed at the appointed time or "when the time came." I believe the time has come for just that. So let's trace the secrets, parables, dreams and riddles through scripture to see what is said about the saints, the cloud of witnesses past and present, that shall be revealed in unity and power in the days to come.

Who are the spiritual children of Abraham with kingdom promise and how shall these things come to pass? Many of the answers are hidden in similes, metaphors and riddles that can be traced through scripture beginning at the beginning.

The LORD told Moses that He speaks to His prophets through visions, dreams and riddles. Jesus explained why this is so (*Numbers 12:6-8; Matthew 13:13*). Follow, then, this riddle: Abraham's descendants would be as numerous as the **stars** (*Genesis 22:17-18*). They would **shine** *like the brightness of the heavens turning many to righteousness* (*Daniel 12:3*). They would be **judges** (**1 Corinthians 6:2**), **kings** and **priests** (*1 Peter 2:9; Revelation 20:4*), being revealed as a **cloud** *of witnesses* through which the Lamb of God lives and reveals Himself from heaven through believers (*back then following a **cloud** by day and a pillar of **fire** by night, now being revealed **with Christ within** (Exodus 13:21; Numbers 14:14; John 14:23; Colossians 1:27*) **with judgment of unbelievers** and the wicked (John 3:16-18), those who follow after the flesh (*Galatians 5:19-21; Hebrews 11-12:1; John 1:29; 3:16-18; Jude 1:14-16; Revelation 14:14-16*). They would be the **house** and **city** of **living stones** (*1 Peter 2:4-5*), not built by human hands, a **city** on a hill (*Matthew 5:13-15*), speaking with the **fire**, the Word (**Sword** of the Spirit), **hammer** of God and **rod of iron** (*Jeremiah 23:29; 2 Peter 3:7; Ephesians 6:17; Hebrews 4:12; Revelation 1:6; 2:16-27; 19:15; Psalm 2; Revelation 2:27; 12:5; 19:15*) of the written and living Word of God (*John 1:1-4; Revelation 1:16; 2:16; 19:15-21*). Their words *are a **tree of life*** (*Proverbs 3:18; 11:30; 15:4 Revelation 22:2-14*), since they are **grafted into the *True Vine*** yielding the fruit of the Spirit (*John 15; Galatians 5:22-23*). They **overcome** the world and the things of the world, becoming the ***New Jerusalem coming down*** *from heaven* (*Revelation 3:12*) and **revealed from heaven**, for the **Father reveals truth from above** (*John 8:23; James 1:17*). They are the **laborers** in the field of harvest **at the end of the age** (*Matthew 13:39; Joel 3:13; Revelation 14:15*). They are **like the ten virgins waiting for their bridegroom to take them to the wedding feast to feast upon and destroy all evil and take hold of their promised inheritance** (*Matthew 25:1-13; Revelation 19:17-19*). They would **throw the dragnet** and **separate the good fish from the bad fish** (*Matthew 13:47-48*). From their bellies **living water**, the Word and the Spirit, would flow like a *river* (*John 4:14; 7:38; Revelation 22:2*). They will **rebuke the nations that delight in war** (*Psalm 9:5; 94:10; Isaiah 17:13*). They will **stand in and possess the gates of the cities of their enemies** (*Genesis 22:17*) and **rebuke the judges** that rejected the Rock, the ones that the builders rejected (*1 Peter 2:6-7*).

"It may seem absurd to you that all these scriptures would refer to the time of renewal. At first glance, I would have to agree. However, I would also have to consider that the "Song of Moses" is mentioned in Deuteronomy *and* Revelation. I would have to also consider that the "harvest" was prophesied by Joel, Jesus and found in Revelation. That thread runs through scripture. So, before you toss this book aside, come and sit down with me and let us consider it together. It may take a while, but I assure you it will be worth your time.

Not every verse has been perfectly clear and I am not a scholar. I have learned that God spoke in visions, dreams, riddles and secrets (*Numbers 12:6-8; Proverbs 1:6; Proverbs 25:2; Matthew 13:9-11*). The overall principles in the Holy Scriptures point to two things: first, to the bruising and lifting up of the Messiah so that mankind may have peace with God through Messiah (*Genesis 3:15; Isaiah 53; Romans 5; John 3:16-18; 12:32*); and second, to the promise that the spiritual children of Abraham, Isaac and Jacob, the followers of the Messiah who died for the sins of the world, must unite as one body (*John 17:23 AMP*) to convince the nations with the commands of Jesus—loving one another with unselfish concern and persuading those who do not believe (*John 13:35; 2 Corinthians 5:11; Psalms 149; Jude 1*).

Some things in this book are old and familiar, while other things are new. *"He said to them, 'Therefore every scribe who has become a disciple of the kingdom of heaven is like the head of a household, who brings out of his treasure things that are new and fresh and things that are old and familiar'"(Matthew 13:52 AMP)*. Consider that even the angels can be misguided:

"God puts no trust or confidence, even in His [heavenly] servants, And He charges His angels with error" (Job 4:18

AMP).

You are His kings and priests; it is to your glory to search these things out with me and glorify the Father and bring all things under Jesus' feet.

♫ **Pause and listen to *End of the Age: Book One, "Old and New" and "Visions and Dreams."*** ♫

Unity is required before the fullness of harvest can come

*"I in them and You in Me, that they may be perfected
and completed into **one**, **so that the world may know
[without any doubt]** that You sent Me, and [that You]
have loved them, just as You have loved Me"*
(John 17:23 AMP).

*"But the natural [unbelieving] man does not accept the
things [the teachings and revelations] of the Spirit of God,
for they are foolishness [absurd and illogical] to him; and he
is incapable of understanding them, because they are spiritually discerned and appreciated, [and he is unqualified to
judge spiritual matters]"*
(1 Corinthians 2:14 AMP).

*"But the Helper (Comforter, Advocate, Intercessor-Coun-
selor, Strengthener, Standby), the Holy Spirit, whom the
Father will send in My name [in My place, to represent Me
and act on My behalf], He will teach you all things. And
He will help you remember everything that I have told you"*
(John 14:26 AMP).

*"It is the glory of God to conceal a matter, **But the glory of
kings is to search out a matter**"*
(Proverbs 25:2 AMP).

Let everything that has breath praise the Lord! Amen!

To the Lord Almighty, keeper of all the keys of our understanding: may
You enlighten all who read this book. Open the secrets to our understanding. Bring along our side your Holy Spirit and great counselors as
we seek to do your will in this hour of trouble when we need you most.

"I bless you, O Son of God, that there is no need for me to
go up to heaven to bring you down or into your grave to
bring you up. You are here, in this hour and at this place.
I confess you as Lord and believe in my heart that you are
risen from the dead."
F.B. Meyer

The time has come... "To execute on them the judgement written. This is the honor for all His godly ones. Praise the LORD! (Hallelujah!)" (*Psalms 149:9 AMP*).

♫ **Pause and listen to** *End of the Age: Book One, "As it is Written."* ♫

Open letter to those who fight against Isaac and Jacob

To all who fight against the sons of Isaac and Jacob write: do you not know that the law of the Spirit of Adoption in Christ by grace is stronger than blood and the laws of blessing and cursing? Do you not know that it was Isaac who was the child of promise through which the Messiah would be born? For Christ, the spotless Lamb, became a curse for us on the tree to bring us to the Father through the torn veil of His body giving us access to the Father. By Him we receive the Spirit of adoption to sonship by which we cry, "Abba, Father" (Romans 8:15). "Jesus said to him, 'I am the [only] Way [to God] and the [real] Truth and the [real] Life; no one comes to the Father but through Me" (John 14:6 AMP).

Truth is not relative. Feelings are relative. The King Solomon speaks of the danger of following our feelings: "There is a way which seems right to a man and appears straight before him, but its end is the way of death" (Proverbs 14:12 AMP). Consider that... "Whatever you hold as your highest good and guiding star is your god" (Jonathan P.). It may be "good" in some way, perhaps in the eyes of some men, but it will be your tyrant if it is not in service to the Creator and His precepts. There must be a balance between the things of this world which are transitory and service to our Maker which carries with it an eternal reward. We must use things to serve man, our families and others in need. We must consider setting right our priorities as described in Proverbs 24. For we are but stewards and we will have to give an account for what we have done and said (Matthew 12:36; Matthew 25:14-46; Romans 14:12). Man has never been able to govern himself for very long. It always ends in chaos and mutual destruction as we see today and in history. We are not commanded to serve ourselves with all our hearts, soul and mind—that is the sin of the evil one, namely to exalt the self above all else (Isaiah 14:14). He tempts us all to do the same. He tempts us with sins of the flesh, violence, power, religious abuses and war. The great Tempter tempts us to control things and people rather than to submit to our Maker. We are commanded to love God with all our heart, soul and mind and to love our neighbor as ourselves (Matthew 22:37-39). Upon these two commands hinge the law and the prophets. Yet most have never understood. The nations are being shaken. Yet this was prophesied as well. The great shaking occurs so that that which cannot be shaken may remain (Hebrews 12:27). Perhaps when we reach the end of our hope we will cry out to the God of Abraham and repent. For as we have done unto those among us—such as the orphans, widows, the poor, and the prisoners—we have done so unto the King, just as it is written (Matthew 25:40). In this way we will be judged.

♫ **Pause and listen to *End of the Age: Book Five, "True Religion."*** ♫

"They who sow in tears shall reap with joyful singing"
(Psalm 126:5).

"I have faith in the people. They will not consent to dis-union. The danger is, they are misled. Let them know the truth, and the country is safe."
Abraham Lincoln

"And if those days [of tribulation] had not been cut short, no human life would be saved; but for the sake of the elect (God's chosen ones) those days will be shortened"
(Matthew 24:22 AMP).

The teachings of the Holy Scriptures repeat themselves from beginning to end lest we forget. That is what a teacher does. The kingdom precepts repeat so we will remember. I am first and foremost a teacher.

The main repeating principle in this book is what happens in the city gate in Proverbs 24:7, Genesis 22:17, and Revelation: The rulers sat in the city gate. Abraham was promised that his descendants would possess the gates of their enemies (i.e. they would judge and rule them).

"Do you not know that the saints [God's people] will [one day] judge the world? If the world is to be judged by you, are you not competent to try trivial [insignificant, petty] cases?" (1 Corinthians 6:2 AMP).

♫ **Pause and listen to** *End of the Age: Book One, "Reserved";*
and End of the Age: Book Two, "Strength for the Harvest", "Leave the Temple"
and "The Dragnet." ♫

Three Daily Prayers by F.B. Meyer

The following three selected prayers come from the November selection of *Pocket Book of Daily Prayers* by F.B. Meyer. These prayers were read on the three different days indicated, as prompted by the Spirit. They match the purposes of this book and the testimony of the author. I was led to open the prayer book on those dates and those dates only while preparing this book.

November 19: Heavenly Father, bring the reign of your Son in every land; may all rulers fall down before Him, all nations serve him. Let His name endure forever, and be continued as long as the sun, and all mankind be blessed in Him.

November 1: Gracious Lord, forgive the past. Keep me as the apple of your eye. Surround me with your guardian care, and let your highest purposes be realized in me. So will I offer in your tabernacle sacrifices of joy. I will sing, yes, I will sing praises to the Lord.

November 24: Holy Father, I mourn the divisions which divide your people, and humbly ask you to fulfill the prayer of our blessed Lord [John 17:23 AMP], that those whom he purchased for his possession may all be one, even as you, Father, are in him and he is in you.

Imagine for a moment that the kingdom promises to Abraham (in Genesis 22), where God promises the gates of justice to his descendants, is woven through the scriptures all the way to Revelation. If that is the case, and it is, then the time of its revelation is in the "time of trouble" spoken of by Jeremiah, at the time Jesus called the *end of the age*. It is the time when *renewal* begins (Matthew 19:28 AMP).

Strengthen your feeble arms and make sturdy your weak knees. Mend your nets with me now and see: cast them into the sea. For every cord in the net is a precept, and every knot a judgment. The LORD Almighty will make you strong. The time fast approaches to cast the dragnet (Matthew 13:47-48).

The Standing Dominos of Kingdom Promises soon to fall

The Lord brought to my remembrance recently a simple game that my brothers and I used to play as children to entertain ourselves. For some it is even a complex competitive sport: practicing the domino effect with dominos while creating complex patterns. The domino effect can also take place in nature and in geopolitical affairs. We, and others of the sport, line up dominos on end and create elaborate lines of arranged dominos, carefully spaced, standing upright. A fractal shape is set up where the first line of dominos splits off the main line of dominos into complex branching patterns. When the critical moment arrives, one domino is tipped forward against the others. What happens next is not easy to guess, provided the creator of the project has been very careful and the dominos don't miss their target when they fall forward.

This book communicates a message similar in nature to that of falling dominos. Our Creator has set in place a series of dominos in the Bible that deal with two agendas He has for the earth: one agenda for the faithful and believing and one agenda for the wicked, oppressive, offensive, sinful, unbelieving, proud and stiff-necked. The first domino was placed in the life of Abraham as a promise. His seed would possess the "gates" of his enemies (Genesis 3:15; 22:17-18). With that domino was an additional promise that through his seed all nations would be blessed (Genesis 12:2-3). Farther down the line in the row of dominos is one mentioned by the prophet Daniel that we consider in this text:

"Those who are wise will shine like the brightness of the heavens, and those who lead many to righteousness, like the stars for ever and ever" (Daniel 12:3 AMP).

Yet another domino is mentioned by Jesus:

> *"So it will be at the end of the age; the angels will come and separate the wicked from the righteous and throw the wicked into the furnace of fire" (Matthew 13:49 AMP).*

The final dominos are mentioned by the Apostle Paul and by John:

A part of this process is to publically denounce and rebuke the wicked.

> *"But to those **[honorable judges] who <u>rebuke</u> the wicked**, it will go well with them and they will find delight, And a good blessing will come upon them" (Proverbs 24:25 AMP).*

> "Who are the honorable judges? Are they only those that hold office? Of course not. Paul said that the saints would judge the world" (*1 Corinthians 6:2*).

It is the purpose of this book to set forth the clear line of dominos for these two agendas and make them easily visible and understandable from Genesis to Revelation. The author hopes that the reader will see them and follow them to their full end so that at the appointed time they can be set into motion with a united body of Christ (John 17:23). For there is an appointed time for every season under the heavens.

> *"There is a season (a time appointed) for everything and a time for every delight and event or purpose under heaven" (Ecclesiastes 3:1 AMP).*

> *"A time to tear apart and a time to sew together; A time to keep silent and a time to speak. A time to love and a time to hate; A time for war and a time for peace" (Ecclesiastes 3:7-8 AMP).*

The time to keep silent has ended. The time has come to speak. The time has come to bind the wicked with the net of their own works by the flame of God's word and His sword of judgement.

> *"That which is has already been, and that which will be has already been before, for God seeks what has passed by [so that history repeats itself]. Moreover, I have seen under the sun that **in the place of justice there is wickedness, and in the place of righteousness there is wickedness.** I said to myself, '**God will judge both the righteous and the wicked,' for there is a time [appointed] for every matter and for every deed**" (Ecclesiastes 3:15-17 AMP).*

> *"Do not think that I have come to bring peace on the earth; I have not come to bring peace, but **a sword [of division between belief and unbelief]**" (Matthew 10:34 AMP).*

> *"From His mouth comes a sharp sword (His word) with which He may strike down the nations, and He will rule them with a rod of iron; and He will tread the wine press of the fierce wrath of God, the Almighty [in judgment of the rebellious world]" (Revelation 19:15 AMP).*

> *"Will He do this alone? No. For we are Christ's body and seated with Him in the heavenlies"* (Ephesians 2:6; 4:25).

The kingdom promises in the Bible spiral upward toward this specific end. While they include both short term and long term prophecies—some fulfilled and others not yet fulfilled—the fullness of the kingdom promises related to the Lord's Prayer and the promises to Abraham are arriving soon. The kingdom promises initiated in Genesis chapter three and in the life of Abraham in Genesis chapter 22 repeat throughout the Bible and hinge on David (2 Samuel 7), the prophets, and Jesus Christ. Jesus said that the harvest of that kingdom promise and mystery occurs at the end of the age (Matthew 13:39; Revelation 10:7). The kingdom promise of the saints' inheritance in the earth comes to pass suddenly at that time of the end and begins the time of renewal that Jesus spoke about. In the beginning they had to be taken on faith; at the end they are taken by force and revelation of the fire and sword of Truth.

The Seven Voices: a summary and call to action

Voice I: We are receiving a kingdom which cannot be shaken

"Now this [expression], 'Yet once more,' indicates the removal and final transformation of all those things which can be shaken—that is, of that which has been created—so that those things which cannot be shaken may remain. Therefore, since we receive a kingdom which cannot be shaken, let us show gratitude, and offer to God pleasing service and acceptable worship with reverence and awe; for our God is [indeed] a consuming fire" (Hebrews 12:27-29 AMP).

"But understand this, that in the last days dangerous times [of great stress and trouble] will come [difficult days that will be hard to bear]. For people will be lovers of self [narcissistic, self-focused], lovers of money [impelled by greed], boastful, arrogant, revilers, disobedient to parents, ungrateful, unholy and profane, [and they will be] unloving [devoid of natural human affection, calloused and inhumane], irreconcilable, malicious gossips, devoid of self-control [intemperate, immoral], brutal, haters of good" (2 Timothy 3:1-3 AMP).

"'Alas! For that day is great, There is none like it; It is the time of Jacob's [unequaled] trouble, But he will be saved

from it; But they shall serve the Lord their God and [the descendant of] David their King, whom I will raise up for them'" (Jeremiah 30:7, 9 AMP).

Prayerfully consider also Matthew 25:34, Revelation 2:26, and Revelation 3:21.

♫ **Pause and listen to *End of the Age: Book One, "Mountain of His House."*** ♫

Voice II: The end was foretold from the beginning

"Declaring the end and the result from the beginning, And from ancient times the things which have not [yet] been done, Saying, 'My purpose will be established, And I will do all that pleases Me and fulfills My purpose (Isaiah 46:10 AMP)."

♫ **Pause and listen to *End of the Age: Book Two, "From the Beginning."*** ♫

The first and latter kingdom promises:

♫ **Pause and listen to *End of the Age: Book Three, "All Nations Blessed."*** ♫

"And God spoke to Abram saying, 'And I will bless (do good for, benefit) those who bless you, And I will curse [that is, subject to My wrath and judgment] the one who curses (despises, dishonors, has contempt for) you. And in you all the families (nations) of the earth will be blessed'" (Genesis 12:3 AMP). "indeed I will greatly bless you, and I will greatly multiply your descendants like the stars of the heavens and like the sand on the seashore; and your seed shall possess the gate of their enemies [as conquerors]" Genesis 22:17 AMP).

"'Do not be afraid and anxious, little flock, for it is your Father's good pleasure to give you the kingdom'" (Luke 12:32 AMP).

"'and the enemy who sowed them is the devil, and the harvest is the end of the age; and the reapers are angels'" (Matthew 13:39 AMP).

"but when it is time for the trumpet call of the seventh angel, when he is about to sound, then the mystery of God [that is, His hidden purpose and plan] is finished, as He announced the gospel to His servants the prophets" (Revelation 10:7 AMP).

These "angels" are the saints. The kingdom riddles are not about word studies, but about riddles and parables that can be understood in any language (Numbers 12:6-7).

Voice III: The judgment of the wicked is the inheritance and honor of the saints

♫ Pause and listen to *End of the Age: Book Two, "Leave the Temple."* ♫

*"'**Then** the kingdom and the dominion and the greatness of all the kingdoms under the whole heaven **will be given to the people of the saints (believers)** of the Most High; His kingdom will be an **everlasting kingdom**, and all the dominions will serve and obey Him'" (Daniel 7:27 AMP).*

*"Do you not know that the saints (God's people) will [**one day**] judge the world? If the world is to be judged by you, are you not competent to try trivial (insignificant, petty) cases?" (1 Corinthians 6:2 AMP).*

"It was about these people that Enoch, in the seventh generation from Adam, prophesied, when he said, "Look, the Lord came with myriads of His holy ones to execute judgment upon all, and to convict all the ungodly of all the ungodly deeds they have done in an ungodly way, and of all the harsh and cruel things ungodly sinners have spoken against Him." These people are [habitual] murmurers, griping and complaining, following after their own desires [controlled by passion]; they speak arrogantly, [pretending

admiration and] flattering people to gain an advantage" (Jude 1:14-16 AMP).

"For the Lord takes pleasure in His people; He will beautify the humble with salvation. Let the godly ones exult in glory; Let them sing for joy on their beds. Let the high praises of God be in their throats, And a two-edged sword in their hands, To execute vengeance on the nations And punishment on the peoples, To bind their kings with chains And their nobles with fetters of iron, To execute on them the judgment written. This is the honor for all His godly ones. Praise the Lord! (Hallelujah!)" (Psalm 149:4-9 AMP).

"'that they all may be one; just as You, Father, are in Me and I in You, that they also may be one in Us, so that the world may believe [without any doubt] that You sent Me'" (John 17:21 AMP).

Voice IV: Kingdom leadership is raised up and revealed during the time of Jacob's trouble

♫ Pause and listen to *End of the Age: Book Two, "Wrestle in the Night"* and *"I See the Clouds."* ♫

"and He will put the sheep on His right [the place of honor], and the goats on His left [the place of rejection]" (Matthew 25:33 AMP).

"'Alas! for that day is great, There is none like it; It is the time of Jacob's [unequaled] trouble, But he will be saved from it. 'It shall come about on that day,' says the Lord of hosts, 'that I will break the yoke off your neck and I will tear off your bonds and force apart your shackles; and strangers will no longer make slaves of the people [of Israel]. But they shall serve the Lord their God and [the descendant of] David their King, whom I will raise up for them" (Jeremiah 30:7-9 AMP).

Note: The kingdom leadership will be "raised up." Jesus will be revealed from above and through His body the Church. This is because Truth is revealed from the Father from above as we will see later in scripture, some of which is mentioned here. Jesus rules from heaven and is seated at the right hand of the Father. His work is finished. All must kiss and pay respect to the Son, Jesus, so that they do not perish in the way.

> *"I will declare the decree of the Lord: He said to Me, 'You are My Son; This day [I proclaim] I have begotten You. 'Ask of Me, and I will assuredly give [You] the nations as Your inheritance, And the ends of the earth as Your possession. 'You shall break them with a rod of iron; You shall shatter them [in pieces] like earthenware.' Now therefore, O kings, act wisely. Be instructed and take warning, O leaders (judges, rulers) of the earth. Worship the Lord and serve Him with reverence [with aweinspired fear and submissive wonder]; Rejoice [yet do so] with trembling. Kiss (pay respect to) the Son, so that He does not become angry, and you perish in the way, For His wrath may soon be kindled and set aflame. blessed [fortunate, prosperous, and favored by God] are all those who take refuge in Him!" (Psalm 2:7-12 AMP).*

> *"'And he who overcomes [the world through believing that Jesus is the Son of God] and he who keeps My deeds [doing things that please Me] until the [very] end, to him I will give authority and power over the nations; and he shall shepherd and rule them with a rod of iron, as the earthen pots are broken in pieces, as I also have received authority [and power to rule them] from My Father; and I will give him the Morning Star. He who has an ear, let him hear and heed what the Spirit says to the churches'" (Revelation 2:26-29 AMP).*

The verses from Psalm 2 and Revelation 2 are parallel passages speaking of the same person or persons. We must remember that **we** are seated with Him in the heavenlies (Ephesians 2:6 AMP). If indeed the King reigns forever, then it must be Jesus through His body the Church. The Apostle Paul said that the saints would judge the world (1 Corinthians 6). In Revelation 1:6 we read that Jesus has made us to be a kingdom of priests. In 1 Peter 2:9 we read that the saints are a royal priesthood made to show forth the excellencies of him who called us out of darkness into his marvelous light.

The Son says the following to the world:

"'The King will answer and say to them, 'I assure you and most solemnly say to you, to the extent that you did it for one of these brothers of Mine, even the least of them, you did it for Me'" (Matthew 25:40 AMP).

Voice V: The Saints respond to the call of Jesus to participate in the kingdom dragnet

"Your people will offer themselves willingly [to participate in Your battle] in the day of Your power; In the splendor of holiness, from the womb of the dawn, Your young men are to You as the dew" (Psalm 110:3 AMP).

"Then the King will say to those on His right, 'Come, you blessed of My Father [you favored of God, appointed to eternal salvation], inherit the kingdom prepared for you from the foundation of the world'" (Matthew 25:34 AMP).

"'For as in those days before the flood they were eating and drinking, marrying and giving in marriage, until the [very] day when Noah entered the ark, and they did not know or understand until the flood came and swept them all away; so will the coming of the Son of Man be [unexpected judgment]. At that time two men will be in the field; one will be taken [for judgment] and one will be left. Two women will be grinding at the mill; one will be taken [for judgment] and one will be left'" (Matthew 24:38-41 AMP).

"To execute on them the judgment written. This is the honor for all His godly ones. Praise the Lord! (Hallelujah!)" (Psalm 149:9 AMP).

"But Jesus said to him, 'No one who puts his hand to the plow and looks back [to the things left behind] is fit for the kingdom of God'" (Luke 9:62 AMP).

"But my righteous one shall live by faith: And if he shrink back, my soul hath no pleasure in him" (Hebrews 10:38 ASV).

"'Again, the kingdom of heaven is like a dragnet which was lowered into the sea, and gathered fish of every kind, and when it was full, they dragged it up on the beach; and they sat down and sorted out the good fish into baskets, but the worthless ones they threw away. So it will be at the end of the age; the angels will come and separate the wicked from the righteous and throw the wicked into the furnace of fire; in that place there will be weeping [over sorrow and pain] and grinding of teeth [over distress and anger]'" (Matthew 13:47-50 AMP).

The furnace is the Word of God which is a consuming fire. It shall test the works of all men.

Voice VI: The books will be opened and their secrets revealed

"It is the glory of God to conceal a matter, But the glory of kings is to search out a matter" (Proverbs 25:2 AMP).

You are His kings and priests. Search out these things to see if they be true or not. Test all things; hold on to that which is good. The "seals" and riddles within the scroll of God's Word that keep us from understanding must be *"opened"* and *"unlocked"* so we can *see with spiritual eyes* and understand.

First, the books were closed and sealed *until* the time of the end. This is part of God's purpose to require faith and keep His Word until the end.

*"The entire vision [of all these things] will be to you **like the words of a scroll that is sealed**, which they give to one who can read, saying, **'Read this, please,'** he shall say, **'I cannot, for it is sealed'"** (Isaiah 29:11 AMP).*

The scroll is sealed to our understanding *until* the end of time.

> *"But as for you, Daniel, **conceal** these words and **seal up the scroll until the end of time**. Many will go back and forth and search anxiously [through the scroll], and knowledge [of the purpose of God as revealed by His prophets] will [greatly] increase" (Daniel 12:4 AMP).*

> *"but **when it is time** for the trumpet call of the seventh angel, when he is about to sound, **then the mystery of God [that is, His hidden purpose and plan] is finished**, as He announced the gospel to His servants the prophets" (Revelation 10:7 AMP).*

> *"Then **He opens the ears of men And seals their instruction.**" (Job 33:16 AMP)*

♫ **Pause and listen to *End of the Age: Book One*, "Old and New."** ♫

Voice VII: Songs in the Night

> *"My mouth will speak wisdom, And the meditation of my heart will be understanding. I will incline my ear and consent to a proverb; On the lyre I will unfold my riddle. Why should I fear in the days of evil, When the wickedness of those who would betray me surrounds me [on every side]" (Psalm 49:3-5 AMP).*

> *"You have held my eyelids open; I am so troubled that I cannot speak. I have considered the ancient days, The years [of prosperity] of long, long ago. I will remember my song in the night; I will meditate with my heart, And my spirit searches" (Psalm 77:4-6 AMP).*

> *"Your statutes are my songs In the house of my pilgrimage" (Psalm 119:54 AMP).*

I pray that you are good soil, that you have ears to hear and that you will bear much fruit. The main precepts in this book were first revealed to me as songs as I searched the scriptures for over two decades. I am sure that other musicians have been inspired by these verses as well. I do not claim to believe that the "songs in the night" reference refers specifically to me. I have only been inspired by them and encouraged by the songs the Lord gave me. As for the songs I wrote, they are not perfect. The lyrics, Biblical concepts, scriptural ideas and testimony is what is important. So be encouraged by them. Encourage one another. Watch, prepare, pray.

Foreword

"The wind blows where it wishes and you hear its sound, but you do not know where it is coming from and where it is going; so it is with everyone who is born of the Spirit" (John 3:8 AMP).

Hopefully, we can all bear and come together to share in the fullness of our inheritance in Christ in the earth at this hour. **It is not about our rescue by a supernatural disappearing act; it is about the saints, in a unified fashion, casting the dragnet and judging the wicked and casting the dragnet just as we have been commanded.**

*"'I have many more things to say to you, but you cannot bear [to hear] them now. But when He, the Spirit of Truth, comes, He will guide you into all the truth [full and complete truth]. For He will not speak on His own initiative, but He will speak whatever He hears [from the Father—the message regarding the Son], and **He will disclose to you what is to come [in the future]. He will glorify and honor Me, because He (the Holy Spirit) will take from what is Mine and will disclose it to you'"** (John 16:12-14 AMP).*

"So we have the prophetic word made more certain. You do well to pay [close] attention to it as to a lamp shining in a dark place, until the day dawns and light breaks through the gloom and the morning star arises in your hearts. But understand this first of all, that no prophecy of Scripture is

a matter of or comes from one's own [personal or special] interpretation, for no prophecy was ever made by an act of human will, but men moved by the Holy Spirit spoke from God" (2 Peter 1:19-21 AMP).

"I sought the LORD [on the authority of His word], and He answered me, And delivered me from all my fears" (Psalm 34:4 AMP).

Now let us begin.

♫ **Pause and listen to *End of the Age: Book Two, "I Will Arise."*** ♫

HARVEST OF THRONES FOR THE RIGHTEOUS

Precept 1: The End Prophecy of Isaiah and the Dreams, Riddles and Secrets spoken to Moses

"And He said, 'Hear now My words: If there is a prophet among you, I the Lord will make Myself known to him in a vision And I will speak to him in a dream. But it is not so with My servant Moses; He is entrusted and faithful in all My house. With him I speak mouth to mouth [directly], Clearly and openly and not in riddles; And he beholds the form of the Lord. Why then were you not afraid to speak against My servant Moses?'" (Numbers 12:6-8 AMP).

"It was because an extraordinary spirit, knowledge and insight, the ability to interpret dreams, clarify riddles, and solve complex problems were found in this Daniel, whom the king named Belteshazzar. Now let Daniel be called and he will give the interpretation" (Daniel 5:12 AMP).

"This is the reason I speak to the crowds in parables: because while [having the power of] seeing they do not see, and while [having the power of] hearing they do not hear, nor do they understand and grasp [spiritual things]. In them the prophecy of Isaiah is being fulfilled, which says, 'You will hear and keep on hearing, but never understand; And you will look and keep on looking, but never comprehend" (Matthew 13:13-14 AMP).

"For now [in this time of imperfection] we see in a mirror dimly [a blurred reflection, a riddle, an enigma], **but then [when the time of perfection comes we will see reality] face to face.** *Now I know in part [just in fragments], but then I will know fully, just as I have been fully known [by God]" (1 Corinthians 13:12 AMP).*

"The secret [of the wise counsel] of the LORD is for those who fear Him, And He will let them know His covenant and reveal to them [through His word] its [deep, inner] meaning" *(Psalm 25:14 AMP).*

"I will incline my ear and consent to a proverb; On the lyre I will unfold my riddle" (Psalm 49:4 AMP).

"Visions, dreams and riddles" (Numbers 12:6-8) are seldom, if at all, interpreted literally. I used to do Greek and Hebrew word studies when analyzing scripture. If we consider how Joseph and Daniel interpreted dreams, along with the fact that God himself says He speaks in riddles, dreams, visions and parables when He speaks through a prophet, then I don't see how a word study is going to get me as far in my spiritual enlightenment with the LORD. Don't get me wrong. I have done and heard word studies that have benefited and edified me spiritually, such as "if anyone is in Christ they are a *new* creation," and "baptized *into* the name of the Father, Son and Holy Spirit." Those who believe *into* Him are adopted by Him and receive the Spirit of Sonship.

Word studies have their place. But in this book I will be teaching and opening the kingdom riddles from Genesis to Revelation, as the Holy Spirit has been teaching me these last twenty-four years.

In order to "riddle out" the secrets of the kingdom of heaven come to earth, I have found that the comparative approach—in which one concept, word or phrase is compared to similar words or phrases in other places in the Bible—seems to work best. It is this comparative approach (midrashic) that has revealed to me many kingdom secrets and mysteries that the body of Christ must know to be prepared for harvest and to understand how to take possession of their inheritance at the time of the consummation of all things and the time of renewal.

"Then the King will say to those on His right, 'Come, you blessed of My Father [you favored of God, appointed to

eternal salvation], inherit the kingdom prepared for you from the foundation of the world'" (Matthew 25:34 AMP).

It is my purpose to let scripture interpret scripture by comparing passages and phrases from Genesis to Revelation that deal with the kingdom as they relate to the promised kingdom, harvest, judgment of the wicked and the inheritance of the saints. This is because these things were repeated throughout the Bible. Consider a verse from the "end of the books" from Revelation:

*"but when it is time for the trumpet call of the seventh angel, when he is about to sound, **then the mystery of God [that is, His hidden purpose and plan] is finished, as He announced the gospel to His servants the prophets"** (Revelation 10:7 AMP).*

This hidden purpose, hidden in the riddles of scripture was repeated from the beginning. It will reveal the details of the coming renewal spoken of by Jesus Christ. In the passage below Jesus speaks of the coming renewal and of other future disciples who will judge the twelve tribes of Israel.

♫ **Pause and listen to *End of the Age: Book Three, "Renewal."*** ♫

"Jesus said to them, 'I assure you and most solemnly say to you, in the renewal [that is, the Messianic restoration and regeneration of all things] when the Son of Man sits on His glorious throne, you [who have followed Me, becoming My disciples] will also sit on twelve thrones, judging the twelve tribes of Israel'" (Matthew 19:28 AMP).

Two primary principles are addressed in the renewal and restoration: 1) the righteous will possess the gates of justice and 2) the knowledge of God and His word will cover the earth as a consuming fire for the wicked and a life-giving sea of water to the rest who believe and are refreshed. Scripture makes clear that the wicked will not understand.

"They will neither harm nor destroy on all my holy mountain, for the earth will be filled with the knowledge of the LORD as the waters cover the sea" (Isaiah 11:9 AMP).

"For the earth will be filled with the knowledge of the glory of the LORD as the waters cover the sea" (Habakkuk 2:14 AMP).

Included among the many things you will read here are the two bookends of the tree of life, one in Genesis and one in Revelation, with several other references to the tree of life in between that give us understanding as to what the tree of life actually is. It is a metaphor for the tree of God that gives life to all who partake of its fruit.

"indeed I will greatly bless you, and I will greatly multiply your descendants like the stars of the heavens and like the sand on the seashore; and your seed shall possess the gate of their enemies [as conquerors]" (Genesis 22:17 AMP).

The time of the end and the renewal is when the righteous are in authority and become great rulers in the earth. The wicked are cast down from their seats of authority.

"When the righteous are in authority and become great, the people rejoice; But when the wicked man rules, the people groan and sigh" (Proverbs 29:2 AMP).

His holy mountain is His chosen nation through which He has chosen to bless the earth. While this is true on one hand, scripture points out that because Israel rejected the Messiah at his first advent, the kingdom will be taken from Israel and given to a nation showing the fruit of repentance (Matthew 21:43).

All of this occurs at the time of the *end*

All of this happens at the *end*. It happens quickly in a time in the earth Jesus refers to as the *renewal* and *harvest*. Jesus said in the parable of the sower that the harvest was the end of the age. On that day the righteous and meek inherit the earth, just as David, the prophets and Jesus foretold. This is when the righteous, in unity, stand in the city gates, the courts of the land, and take possession of them and rebuke the wicked with the fire of the Word of God, the judgment written, that has come true for the righteous as well as for the wicked. The parable of the dragnet comes to pass at that time.

Today the city gates are ruled by the wicked. We are divided and are looking to the clouds and perfect conditions before we act instead of to the Word of God for answers. Do not despair. Those who have kept their lamps burning will be ready. Just as we were taught to pray in the Lord's Prayer, so will God's will be done in the earth.

"He said to them, 'When you pray, say: 'Father hallowed be Your name. Your kingdom come' (Luke 11:2 AMP).

Through the prophets God declared the end of the matter from the beginning

"Declaring the end and the result from the beginning, And from ancient times the things which have not [yet] been done, Saying, 'My purpose will be established, And I will do all that pleases Me and fulfills My purpose'" (Isaiah 46:10 AMP).

Solomon's warning about those who will not reap a harvest

"He who watches the wind [waiting for all conditions to be perfect] will not sow [seed], and he who looks at the clouds will not reap [a harvest]" (Ecclesiastes 11:4 AMP).

The Son of Man (Jesus) is manifest *within* or *as* a cloud of saints in the earth. I am only His bondservant.

This is probably one of the greater riddles of scripture.

"Immediately after the tribulation of those days the sun will be darkened, and the moon will not provide its light, and the stars will fall from the sky, and the powers of the heavens will be shaken. And at that time the sign of the Son of Man [coming in His glory] will appear in the sky, and then all the tribes of the earth [and especially Israel] will mourn [regretting their rebellion and rejection of the Messiah], and they will see the Son of Man coming on the clouds of heaven with power and great glory [in brilliance and splendor]. And He will send His angels with a loud trumpet and they will gather together His elect (God's chosen ones) from the four winds, from one end of the heavens to the other. At that time two men will be in the field; one will be [taken [for judgment] and one will be left. Two women will be grinding at the mill; one will be taken [for judgment] and one will be left" (Matthew 24:29-31; 40-41 AMP).*

On the clouds of *heaven* refers to the saints whose citizenship is in heaven. This will become more evident to you as you continue reading. It is one of the riddles of the kingdom of heaven. For Christ's followers are seated with Him in the heavenlies now and share His authority to rule with Him (Ephesians 2:6 AMP). They-we- should be exercising it in unity instead of waiting for His rescue.

Consider what the prophet Samuel said,

"The LORD makes poor and makes rich; He brings low and He lifts up. 'He raises up the poor from the dust, He lifts up the needy from the ash heap to make them sit with nobles, And inherit a seat of honor and glory; For the pillars of the earth are the LORD'S, And He set the land on them. 'He will guard the feet of His godly (faithful) ones, But the wicked ones are silenced and perish in darkness; For a man shall not prevail by might"' (1 Samuel 2:7-9).

We are his cloud of witnesses, and He is in us

"It was about these people that Enoch, in the seventh gen-

8

*eration from Adam, prophesied, when he said, 'Look, **the Lord came with myriads of His holy ones to execute judgment upon** all, and to convict all the ungodly of all the ungodly deeds they have done in an ungodly way, and of all the harsh and cruel things ungodly sinners have spoken against Him.' These people are [habitual] murmurers, griping and complaining, following after their own desires [controlled by passion]; they speak arrogantly, [pretending admiration and] flattering people to gain an advantage"* (Jude 1:14-16 AMP).

Many will be purified, but none of the wicked will understand

"Many will be purged, purified (made white) and refined, but the wicked will behave wickedly. None of the wicked shall understand, but those who are [spiritually] wise will understand" (Daniel 12:10 AMP).

The apostle Paul explained the mystery for the rejection of the Messiah.

"Then appreciate the gracious kindness and the severity of God: to those who fell [into spiritual ruin], severity, but to you, God's gracious kindness—if you continue in His kindness [by faith and obedience to Him]; otherwise you too will be cut off. And even they [the unbelieving Jews], if they do not continue in their unbelief, will be grafted in; for God has the power to graft them in again. For if you were cut off from what is by nature a wild olive tree, and against nature were grafted into a cultivated olive tree, how much easier will it be to graft these who are the natural branches back into [the original parent stock of] their own olive tree? I do not want you, believers, to be unaware of this mystery [God's previously hidden plan]—so that you will not be wise in your own opinion—that a partial hardening has [temporarily] happened to Israel [to last] until the full number of the Gentiles has come in; and so [at that time] all Israel [that is, all Jews who have a personal faith in Jesus as Messiah] will be saved; just as it is written [in Scripture],'The Deliverer (Messiah) will come from Zion, He will remove ungodliness

from Jacob' 'This is My covenant with them, When I take away their sins.' From the standpoint of the gospel, the Jews [at present] are enemies [of God] for your sake [which is for your benefit], but from the standpoint of God's choice [of the Jews as His people], they are still loved by Him for the sake of the fathers. For the gifts and the calling of God are irrevocable [for He does not withdraw what He has given, nor does He change His mind about those to whom He gives His grace or to whom He sends His call]. Just as you once were disobedient and failed to listen to God, but have now obtained mercy because of their disobedience, so they too have now become disobedient so that they too may one day receive mercy because of the mercy shown to you. For God has imprisoned all in disobedience so that He may show mercy to all [Jew and Gentile alike]. Oh, the depth of the riches and wisdom and knowledge of God! How unsearchable are His judgments and decisions and how unfathomable and untraceable are His ways! For who has known the mind of the Lord, or who has been His counselor? Or who has first given to Him that it would be paid back to him? For from Him [all things originate] and through Him [all things live and exist] and to Him are all things [directed]. To Him be glory and honor forever! Amen" (Romans 11:22-36 AMP).

♫ Pause and listen to *End of the Age: Book Four, "Gifts and Callings."* ♫

The Deception of God

♫ Pause and listen to *End of the Age: Book Two, "Grafted."* ♫

God does permit the wicked to fall headlong into self-deception. He tells us that they will be caught in their own net:

> *"The violence of the wicked will [return to them and] drag them away [like fish caught in a net],* **Because they refuse to act with justice**" *(Proverbs 21:7 AMP).*

He will even deceive His own servants if it serves His purposes (Jeremiah 20:7). Jesus spoke in veiled speech when he used parables to teach.

Remember when His disciples asked him why he spoke in parables? Consider His reply:

> *"And He said, 'To you [who have been chosen] it has been granted to know and recognize the mysteries of the kingdom of God, but to the rest it is in parables, so that though seeing they may not see, and hearing they may not understand"'* *(Luke 8:10 AMP).*

> *"For God has put in their hearts to carry out His purpose by agreeing together to surrender their kingdom to the beast, until the [prophetic] words of God will be fulfilled"* *(Revelation 17:17 AMP).*

I highly recommend that you consider the Phillips translation of Revelation 17:16-18 and related commentaries.

The culmination of the kingdom parables is the time of the fulfillment of the kingdom come to earth.

♫ **Pause and listen to *End of the Age: Book One, "I Will Not Trust."*** ♫

Precept 2: Prophecies of the "Latter Days" begin in the books of Moses

The latter days is mentioned a total of nine times in the Books of Moses and the Prophets. Through Isaiah, God said that He has been speaking about the end and culmination of His Word from the very beginning.

> *"Declaring the end and the result from the beginning, And from ancient times the things which have not [yet] been done, Saying, 'My purpose will be established, And I will do all that pleases Me and fulfills My purpose'" (Isaiah 46:10 AMP).*

The first reference to "latter days" is in Deuteronomy chapter four

> *"The Lord will scatter and disperse you among the peoples (pagan nations), and you will be left few in number among the nations where the Lord drives you. And there you will serve [false and foreign] gods, the work of human hands, [lifeless images of] wood and stone, which neither see nor hear nor eat nor smell [the offerings of food given to them]. But from there you will seek the Lord your God, and you will find Him if you search for Him with all your heart and all your soul. When you are in distress and tribulation and all these things come on you, **in the latter days you will re-***

turn to the Lord your God and listen to His voice. For the Lord your God is a merciful and compassionate God; He will not fail you, nor destroy you, nor forget the covenant with your fathers which He swore to them" (Deuteronomy 4:27-31 AMP).

Other references to the "latter days" spoken by Moses and the prophets

*"For I know that **after my death you will behave corruptly and turn from the way which I have commanded you; and evil will come upon you in the latter days, because you will do evil in the sight of the Lord, provoking Him to anger with the work of your hands"** (Deuteronomy 31:29).*

*"The fierce (righteous) anger of the Lord will not turn back Until He has fulfilled and until He has accomplished The intent of His heart (mind); **In the latter days you will understand this"** (Jeremiah 30:24 AMP).*

"But it shall come about in the last days That the mountain of the house of the Lord Shall be established as the highest and chief of the mountains; It shall be above the hills, And peoples shall flow [like a river] to it" (Micah 4:1 AMP).

Beginning in Genesis, we find an important promise in the Abrahamic Covenant

Yet, we can still go back further to the kingdom promises. In Genesis 3 we read of the promised Messiah that would be born of a virgin ("her Seed") and overcome Satan (bruise the serpent's head).

"'And I will put enmity (open hostility) Between you and the woman, And between your seed (offspring) and her Seed; He shall [fatally] bruise your head, And you shall [only] bruise His heel'" (Genesis 3:15 AMP).

Then in Genesis 22 the Angel of the LORD speaks to Abraham after

14

stopping him from sacrificing his son, foreshadowing the once for al
l Passover sacrifice of Jesus Christ. This is what the Angel of the LOR
D says,

> *"indeed I will greatly bless you, and I will greatly multiply
> your descendants **like the stars of the heavens** and like
> the sand on the seashore; and your seed shall possess the gate
> of their enemies [as conquerors]. Through your seed all the
> nations of the earth shall be blessed, because you have heard
> and obeyed My voice" (Genesis 22:17-18 AMP).*

More specific aspects of this promise will be discussed later. Suffice to
say that this promise is ongoing and has not yet reached its culmination.
Also, I should reiterate Isaiah 46:10–that the "end of the matter" has
been told and retold from the very beginning. Even Jesus spoke of this in
the Parable of the Sower. He said the harvest is the end of the age.

> *"He answered, 'The one who sows the good seed is the Son of
> Man, and the field is the world; and [as for] the good seed,
> these are the sons of the kingdom; and the weeds are the sons
> of the evil one; and the enemy who sowed them is the devil,
> and **the harvest is the end of the age; and the reapers
> are angels**. So just as the weeds are gathered up and burned
> in the fire, so will it be at the end of the age. The Son of
> Man will send out His angels, and they will gather out of
> His kingdom all things that offend [those things by which
> people are led into sin], and all who practice evil [leading
> others into sin], and will throw them into the furnace of
> fire; in that place there will be weeping [over sorrow and
> pain] and grinding of teeth [over distress and anger]. **Then
> the righteous [those who seek the will of God] will
> shine forth [radiating the new life] like the sun in
> the kingdom** of their Father. He who has ears [to hear], let
> him hear and heed My words" (Matthew 13:37-43 AMP).*

Consider that there is a global net that the saints, with God's direction,
can exploit for this purpose.

"For the wicked is thrown into a net by his own feet (wicked-ness), And he steps on the webbing [of the lattice covered pit]" (Job 18:8 AMP).

"The nations have sunk down in the pit which they have made; In the net which they hid, their own foot has been caught" (Psalm 9:15 AMP).

"Let the wicked fall into their own nets, While I pass by and safely escape [from danger]" (Psalm 141:10 AMP).

"'Again, the kingdom of heaven is like a dragnet which was lowered into the sea, and gathered fish of every kind, and when it was full, they dragged it up on the beach; and they sat down and sorted out the good fish into baskets, but the worthless ones they threw away'" (Matthew 13:47-48 AMP).

Precept 3: Jesus' High Priestly Prayer for the Saints: unity so the world will believe

The unity of the saints was a critical priority for Jesus' prayer for us in John 17 for the specific purpose of convincing the world.

> *"I do not pray for these alone [it is not for their sake only that I make this request], but also for [all] those who [will ever] believe and trust in Me through their message, that they all may be one; just as You, Father, are in Me and I in You, that they also may be one in Us, so that the world may believe [without any doubt] that You sent Me" (John 17:20-21 AMP).*

The burden of convincing the world falls upon the disciples and their unity. This is the Church, the Body of Christ. **Jesus did not say that He would convince the world. We must consider what Jesus says and also what he does not say in a given passage to avoid confusion. Yes, He will convince the world, but it will be through His body, the Church and the scriptures (Romans 3:31; 2 Timothy 3:16; Jude 1:15).**

This truth is made even clearer when Jesus says He is no longer in the world in verse eleven of John 17.

The Saints bring in the Harvest

The work of harvest is performed by the "angels" or "sons of God," God's servants, His messengers of fire, the saints. Jude discusses the role of the saints in the judgment of the ungodly and the implied call to avoid division.

> *"It was about these people that Enoch, in the seventh generation from Adam, prophesied, when he said, 'Look, the Lord came with myriads of His holy ones to execute judgment upon all, and to convict all the ungodly of all the ungodly deeds they have done in an ungodly way, and of all the harsh and cruel things ungodly sinners have spoken against Him.' These people are [habitual] murmurers, griping and complaining, following after their own desires [controlled by passion]; they speak arrogantly, [pretending admiration and] flattering people to gain an advantage. But as for you, beloved, remember the [prophetic] words spoken by the apostles of our Lord Jesus Christ. They used to say to you, 'In the last days there will be scoffers, following after their own ungodly passions.' These are the ones who are [agitators] causing divisions—worldly-minded [secular, unspiritual, carnal, merely sensual—unsaved], devoid of the Spirit"* (Jude 1:14-19 AMP).

In the same chapter, the wicked are referred to as clouds without rain. In Hebrews chapter twelve we read about the cloud of witnesses, the saints. Conversely, the saints would be clouds with refreshing rain.

As to the messengers of fire...

> *"and to give relief to you who are so distressed and to us as well when the Lord Jesus is revealed from heaven with His mighty angels in a flame of fire"* 2 Thessalonians 1:7 AMP).

From our bellies flows living water (John) and judgment from our mouths. It is His way. It is His riddle, just as He spoke to Jeremiah, John and through Jesus. It is the same riddle, but in reverse: instead of river (water) for life, it is fire for judgment.

In this treaty the fact that spiritual truth is revealed from heaven is addressed.

Again, the call to unity is embedded in Jude 1. Unity is crucial. We are commanded to avoid divisions. Following the unity of the Spirit through the bond of peace is paramount. Do not be divided by tradition or the wicked who tempt, deride and divide you.

> "For He Himself is our peace and our bond of unity. He who made both groups— [Jews and Gentiles]—into one body and broke down the barrier, dividing wall [of spiritual antagonism between us]" (Ephesians 2:14 AMP).

> "Let the godly ones exult in glory; Let them sing for joy on their beds. Let the high praises of God be in their throats, And a twœdged sword in their hands, To execute vengeance on the nations And punishment on the peoples" (Psalm 149:5-7 AMP).

Where God is not feared and there is no revelation of His word, restraint is cast off

> "Where there is no vision [no revelation of God and His word], the people are unrestrained; But happy and blessed is he who keeps the law [of God]" (Proverbs 29:18 AMP).

Yet we have this promise: all will know God

> "And each man will no longer teach his neighbor and his brother, saying, 'Know the Lord,' for they will all know Me [through personal experience], from the least of them to the greatest," says the Lord. "For I will forgive their wickedness, and I will no longer remember their sin" (Jeremiah 31:34 AMP).

Precept 4: The Tree of Life from Genesis to Revelation

♪ Pause and listen to *End of the Age: Book One, "Tree of Life."* ♪

The term *tree of life* is mentioned at the beginning, middle, and end of the scriptures. In Proverbs, Solomon refers to "wisdom" being a tree of life and that the fear of God is the beginning of wisdom. In Psalm 1 the righteous man who does not take counsel with the wicked is like a tree planted by the water that bears fruit in its season. Consider those verses along with the True Vine of Jesus Christ, the Messiah, and that we are grafted into the Vine and now called his branches, His body, and that He is the head of the body, the church. We are salt, we are light, we are like the stars that shine. (John 15, Matthew 5:13-14; Daniel 12:3).

> *"Those who are [spiritually] wise will shine brightly like the brightness of the expanse of heaven, and those who lead many to righteousness, [will shine] like the stars forever and ever"* (Daniel 12:3 AMP).

I would posit, based on the following scriptures, that the righteous are part of the tree of life, those that fear God, rooted in Christ and growing up, every member supporting the other, into the Bride of Christ. Consider the words of Solomon along with John 15 since we are grafted into the vine of Christ.

> *"The fruit of the [consistently] righteous is a tree of life, And*

he who is wise captures and wins souls [for God—he gathers them for eternity]" (Proverbs 11:30 AMP).

Just as Jesus is the True vine, so is He the Tree of Life. Just as we are the branches grafted into the vine, so are we the branches grafted into the tree of life that bear fruit. And remember also we can approach scripture by 1) interpreting exactly what it says in its context, 2) it may conceal a secret, 3) it may be a mystery, a riddle within a riddle, or 4) or make a comparison with similar passages.

The phrase "tree of life" occurs over ten times in the Bible. It is important to look at them together to see the different symbolisms. Looking at all of them in many places and letting scripture interpret scripture gives us an understandable picture.

> *"And [in that garden] the Lord God caused to grow from the ground every tree that is desirable and pleasing to the sight and good (suitable, pleasant) for food; the tree of life was also in the midst of the garden, and the tree of the [experiential] knowledge (recognition) of [the difference between] good and evil" (Genesis 2:9 AMP).*

If you know "good and evil," then the soil of your heart will grow good seed or bad seed. You will be susceptible to the evil one. This is clear in the parable of the sower.

> *"And the Lord God said, 'Behold, the man has become like one of Us (Father, Son, Holy Spirit), knowing [how to distinguish between] good and evil; and now, he might stretch out his hand, and take from the tree of life as well, and eat [its fruit], and live [in this fallen, sinful condition] forever'" (Genesis 3:22 AMP).*

> *"So God drove the man out; and at the east of the Garden of Eden He [permanently] stationed the cherubim and the sword with the flashing blade which turned round and round [in every direction] to protect and guard the way (entrance, access) to the tree of life" (Genesis 3:24 AMP).*

Wisdom is a tree of life

*"She (wisdom) is a tree of life to those who take hold of her,
And happy [blessed, considered fortunate, be admired] is
everyone who holds her tightly" (Proverbs 3:18 AMP).*

But wisdom has to begin somewhere. What does the Bible teach about wisdom?

The fear of the Lord is the beginning of wisdom

*"The [reverent] fear of the Lord is the beginning (the pre-
requisite, the absolute essential, the alphabet) of wisdom;
A good understanding and a teachable heart are possessed
by all those who do the will of the Lord; His praise endures
forever" (Psalm 111:10 AMP).*

*"The [reverent] fear of the Lord [that is, worshiping Him
and regarding Him as truly awesome] is the beginning and
the preeminent part of knowledge [its starting point and
its essence]; But arrogant fools despise [skillful and godly]
wisdom and instruction and self-discipline" (Proverbs 1:7
AMP).*

Up to this point we have seen the tree of life in the garden which leads to life and also that wisdom is considered to be a tree of life for all who take hold of her. If we eat of the fruit of the tree of life, we shall live. Jesus said that any person who believes in Him shall pass from death to life. His words are recorded in the gospel of John:

*"I assure you and most solemnly say to you, the person who
hears My word [the one who heeds My message], and believes and trusts in Him who sent Me, has (possesses now)
eternal life [that is, eternal life actually begins-the believer is transformed], and does not come into judgment and
condemnation, but has passed [over] from death into life"
(John 5:24 AMP).*

23

The fruit of the righteous is a tree of life

"The fruit of the [consistently] righteous is a tree of life, And he who is wise captures and wins souls [for God—he gathers them for eternity]" (Proverbs 11:30 AMP).

"Hope deferred makes the heart sick, But when desire is fulfilled, it is a tree of life" (Proverbs 13:12 AMP).

The desire of the righteous is the coming of the kingdom. Does this mean that the Tree of Life in Revelation relates to the establishment of the promised kingdom in the earth? Perhaps. The desire of the ages, "Thy will be done, in earth as it is in heaven," would indeed be a tree of life in the earth.

A soothing tongue is a tree of life

"A soothing tongue [speaking words that build up and encourage] is a tree of life, But a perverse tongue [speaking words that overwhelm and depress] crushes the spirit" (Proverbs 15:4 AMP).

So the fruit of the righteous is a tree of life. Desire fulfilled is a tree of life and a soothing tongue is a tree of life. In similar poetic language in Jude 1:11-13 we find a contrast between the righteous and the wicked, for they are *"trees without fruit"* and *"clouds without water."*

The wicked are clouds without water and trees without fruit

"Woe to them! For they have gone the [defiant] way of Cain, and for profit they have run headlong into the error of Balaam, and perished in the rebellion of [mutinous] Korah. These men are hidden reefs [elements of great danger to others] in your love feasts when they feast together with you without fear, looking after [only] themselves; [they are like] clouds without water, swept along by the winds; autumn trees without fruit, doubly dead, uprooted and lifeless; wild waves of the sea, flinging up their own shame like foam;

wandering stars, for whom the gloom of deep darkness has been reserved forever" (Jude 1:11-13 AMP).

Who has access to the tree of life?

"'He who has an ear, let him hear and heed what the Spirit says to the churches. To him who overcomes [the world through believing that Jesus is the Son of God], I will grant [the privilege] to eat [the fruit] from the tree of life, which is in the Paradise of God'" (Revelation 2:7 AMP).

"Then the angel showed me a river of the water of life, clear as crystal, flowing from the throne of God and the Lamb (Christ), in the middle of its street. On either side of the river was the tree of life, bearing twelve kinds of fruit, yielding its fruit every month; and the leaves of the tree were for the healing of the nations" (Revelation 22:12 AMP).

"Blessed (happy, prosperous, to be admired) are those who wash their robes [in the blood of Christ by believing and trusting in Him—the righteous who do His commandments], so that they may have the right to the tree of life, and may enter by the gates into the city. Outside are the dogs [the godless, the impure, those of low moral character] and the sorcerers [with their intoxicating drugs, and magic arts], and the immoral persons [the perverted, the molesters, and the adulterers], and the murderers, and the idolaters, and everyone who loves and practices lying (deception, cheating)" (Revelation 22:14-15 AMP).

"and if anyone takes away from or distorts the words of the book of this prophecy, God will take away [from that one] his share from the tree of life and from the holy city (new Jerusalem), which are written in this book" (Revelation 22:19 AMP).

Two of the possible interpretations of scripture discussed in Precept 1 of this book included a secret and a mystery. Jesus referred to himself as the True Vine and the disciples and those that believe in him as the branches that bear fruit (John 15). We have seen that tree of life can reference wisdom, desire fulfilled, a soothing tongue, and the fruit of the righteous. David, in Psalm 1, references a person that doesn't take counsel with the wicked as being like a tree planted by streams of water.

Consider what he says:

> *"Blessed [fortunate, prosperous, and favored by God] is the man who does not walk in the counsel of the wicked [following their advice and example], Nor stand in the path of sinners, Nor sit [down to rest] in the seat of scoffers (ridiculers). But his delight is in the law of the Lord, And on His law [His precepts and teachings] he [habitually] meditates day and night. And he will be like a tree firmly planted [and fed] by streams of water,* **Which yields its fruit in its season***; Its leaf does not wither; And in whatever he does, he prospers [and comes to maturity]" (Psalm 1:1-3 AMP).*

In another place (Isaiah), the word tree is used to refer to people— "trees (or oaks) of righteousness." Their purpose is to glorify God.

> *"To grant to those who mourn in Zion the following: To give them a turban instead of dust [on their heads, a sign of mourning], The oil of joy instead of mourning, The garment [expressive] of praise instead of a disheartened spirit.* **So they will be called the trees of righteousness [strong and magnificent, distinguished for integrity, justice, and right standing with God], The planting of the Lord, that He may be glorified***" (Isaiah 61:3 AMP).*

Don't read this verse lightly. Consider the terminology. Strong. Magnificent. Distinguished for integrity. Justice. Having right standing with God—everything the wicked are not.

We can confidently say that the *Tree of Life* is several things: 1) the fear of God, 2) the fruit of the consistently righteous, 3) a desire fulfilled, and 4) a soothing tongue. We can say confidently that the tree of life in the holy city in Revelation is the fear of God, which is the beginning of wisdom and the fruit of the consistently righteous who honor God's word and execute justice in the earth. It is also the desire of the ages, the inheritance of the kingdom in the earth prophesied by David, Jesus, and referenced

THREE HARVESTS AND THE DRAGNET

by the apostle Paul.

Precept 5: The Holy City of Living Stones

Next question: What—or rather *who*—is the new Jerusalem revealed from heaven (Revelation 21:2)? If you read that verse it sounds like it is referring to the Bride of Christ. Does it have anything to do with the new covenant in the blood and body of Jesus Christ (Luke 22:20)? Does it have anything to do with the God's house made of living stones mentioned by the apostle Peter? We will now consider those questions.

> *"You [believers, like living stones, are being built up into a spiritual house for a holy and dedicated priesthood, to offer spiritual sacrifices [that are] acceptable and pleasing to God through Jesus Christ" (1 Peter 2:4-5 AMP).*

Jeremiah was likened unto **a city, an iron pillar and bronze walls** when God called him to be his mouthpiece and speak against the tribes of Israel regarding judgment:

> *"Now behold, I have made you today like a fortified city and like an iron pillar and like bronze walls against the whole land—against the [successive] kings of Judah, against its leaders, against its priests, and against the people of the land [giving you divine strength which no hostile power can overcome]. They will fight against you, but they will not [ultimately] prevail over you, for I am with you [always] to protect you and deliver you,' says the Lord" (Jeremiah*

29

1:18-19 AMP).

Jesus likened his disciples to a city on a hill. If we compare these passages, we gain new insight into God's intention—a fortified city, giving them divine strength which no hostile power can overcome; the hostile power will not ultimately prevail.

"'You are the light of [Christ to] the world. A city set on a hill cannot be hidden; nor does anyone light a lamp and put it under a basket, but on a lamp stand, and it gives light to all who are in the house. Let your light shine before men in such a way that they may see your good deeds and moral excellence, and [recognize and honor and] glorify your Father who is in heaven'" (Matthew 5:14-16 AMP).

In Revelation we read about the mystery of the New Jerusalem coming down out of heaven:

"And I saw the holy city, new Jerusalem, coming down out of heaven from God, arrayed like a bride adorned for her husband" (Revelation 21:2 AMP).

The writer of Hebrews makes it crystal clear.

"But you have come to Mount Zion and to the city of the living God, the heavenly Jerusalem, and to myriads of angels [in festive gathering], and to the general assembly and assembly of the firstborn who are registered [as citizens] in heaven, and to God, who is Judge of all, and to the spirits of the righteous (the redeemed in heaven) who have been made perfect [bringing them to their final glory], and to Jesus, the Mediator of a new covenant [uniting God and man], and to the sprinkled blood, which speaks [of mercy], a better and nobler and more gracious message than the blood of Abel [which cried out for vengeance]" (Hebrews 12:22-24 AMP).

Truth comes down and is revealed from above

The heavenly Jerusalem is the city of God made with living stones, the saints of God past and present. It is the general assembly of the saints and all of those redeemed. And what does it mean in Revelation 21:2 "coming down out of heaven from God?" It means that Truth is revealed from above, from heaven.

> *"Do not be misled, my beloved brothers and sisters. Every good thing given and **every perfect gift is from above; it comes down from the Father of lights** [the Creator and Sustainer of the heavens], in whom there is no variation [no rising or setting] or shadow cast by His turning [for He is perfect and never changes]. It was of His own will that He gave us birth [as His children] by the word of truth, so that we would be a kind of first fruits of His creatures [a prime example of what He created to be set apart to Himself— sanctified, made holy for His divine purposes]" (James 1:16-18 AMP).*

To be revealed from heaven means that the truth or person(s) in question are revealed by God from heaven. The revelation "comes down from heaven" because the knowledge of God is not earthly, nor is it obtained by natural means. Consider what Jesus said to Peter:

> *"Then Jesus answered him, 'Blessed [happy, spiritually secure, favored by God] are you, Simon son of Jonah, **because flesh and blood (mortal man) did not reveal this to you, but My Father who is in heaven**'" (Matthew 16:17 AMP).*

Does this mean that the new Jerusalem coming down from heaven is the revelation of the Bride of Christ in the earth? Does it mean that the righteous are trees of life bearing the fruit of Christ as His Royal Priesthood carrying forth the message of salvation in the earth? Yes and yes.

31

> *"But you are a chosen race, a royal priesthood, a consecrated nation, a [special] people for God's own possession, so that you may proclaim the excellencies [the wonderful deeds and virtues and perfections] of Him who called you out of darkness into His marvelous light" (1 Peter 2:9 AMP).*

Jesus will be revealed from above with His mighty saints, His angels

Jesus will be revealed from heaven to the earth, because Truth is revealed from above, within his servants, the elect of the kingdom. He will be revealed in flames of fire as mentioned in 2 Thessalonians 1:7.

> *"and to give relief to you who are so distressed and to us as well when the Lord Jesus is revealed from heaven with His mighty angels in a flame of fire" (2 Thessalonians 1:7 AMP).*

If the saints judge the wicked in the last day, and if Jesus comes with His angels, then aren't those the same thing because He lives within us? Some would say no, but I say yes based on what find here.

What is meant by flames of fire? Again, a comparative study will show us.

> *"And concerning the angels He says, 'Who makes His angels winds, And His ministering servants flames of fire [to do His bidding])' (Hebrews 1:7 AMP).*

> *"The wind blows where it wishes and you hear its sound, but you do not know where it is coming from and where it is going; so it is with everyone who is born of the Spirit" (John 3:8 AMP).*

> *"And to the angel (divine messenger) of the church in Thyatira write: 'These are the words of the Son of God, who has eyes [that flash] like a flame of fire [in righteous judgment], and whose feet are like burnished [whitehot] bronze'" (Revelation 2:18 AMP).*

32

Flames of fire refers to judgment and God refers to His word as a consuming fire. Shall Jesus do this bodily and alone when he is revealed? Or is He revealed through the body of His Church, the Bride of Christ, the New Jerusalem? Let us consider several scriptures concerning judgement and the kingdom to answer this question.

Judgment, the Kingdom and Honorable Judges

"It was about these people that Enoch, in the seventh generation from Adam, prophesied, when he said, 'Look, the Lord came with myriads of His holy ones to execute judgment upon all, and to convict all the ungodly of all the ungodly deeds they have done in an ungodly way, and of all the harsh and cruel things ungodly sinners have spoken against Him.' These people are [habitual] murmurers, griping and complaining, following after their own desires [controlled by passion]; they speak arrogantly, [pretending admiration and] flattering people to gain an advantage" (Jude 1:14-16 AMP).

"Do you not know that the saints (God's people) will [one day] judge the world? If the world is to be judged by you, are you not competent to try trivial (insignificant, petty) cases?" (1 Corinthians 6:2 AMP).

"And the nations (Gentiles) became enraged, and Your wrath and indignation came, and the time came for the dead to be judged, and [the time came] to reward Your bondservants the prophets and the saints (God's people) and those who fear Your name, the small and the great, and [the time came] to destroy the destroyers of the earth. And the temple of God which is in heaven was opened; and the ark of His covenant appeared in His temple, and there were flashes of lightning, loud rumblings and peals of thunder and an earthquake and a great hailstorm" (Revelation 11:18 AMP).

"But to those [honorable judges] who rebuke the wicked, it will go well with them and they will find delight, And a good blessing will come upon them" (Proverbs 24:25 AMP).

"Let the godly ones exult in glory; Let them sing for joy on their beds. Let the high praises of God be in their throats,

33

And a twoedged sword in their hands, To execute vengeance on the nations And punishment on the peoples, To bind their kings with chains And their nobles with fetters of iron, To execute on them the judgment written. This is the honor for all His godly ones. Praise the Lord! (Hallelujah!)" (Psalm 149:59 AMP).

Judgment of the wicked is part of the inheritance of the saints

As the Word of God is fulfilled it becomes a fire in the mouths of the saints and a two-edged sword in their hands (Hebrews 4:12). When does this harvest of the inheritance begin? It occurs when the wickedness of the earth has reached its fullness according to the prophet Joel.

"Put in the sickle [of judgment], for the harvest is ripe; Come, tread [the grapes], for the wine press is full; The vats overflow, for the wickedness [of the people] is great. Multitudes, multitudes in the valley of decision (judgment)! For the day of the Lord is near in the valley of decision [when judgment is executed]. The sun and the moon grow dark And the stars lose their brightness. The Lord thunders and roars from Zion And utters His voice from Jerusalem [in judgment of His enemies], And the heavens and the earth tremble and shudder; But the Lord is a refuge for His people And a stronghold [of protection] to the children of Israel. Then you will know and understand fully that I am the Lord your God, Dwelling in Zion, My holy mountain. Then Jerusalem will be holy, And strangers [who do not belong] will no longer pass through it" (Joel 3:13-17 AMP).

"And another angel came from the altar, the one who has power over fire; and he called with a loud voice to him who had the sharp sickle, saying, 'Put in your sharp sickle and reap the clusters of grapes from the vine of the earth, because her grapes are ripe [for judgment]'" (Revelation 14:18 AMP).

The "fire" is the Word of God and the sickle is His Word purposed for judgment

> *"But God will shoot them with an [unexpected] arrow; Suddenly they will be wounded. So they will be caused to stumble; their own tongue is against them; All who gaze at them will shake the head [in scorn]" (Psalms 64:7-8 AMP).*

> *"God [in His eternal plan] chose to make known to them how great for the Gentiles are the riches of the glory of this mystery, which is Christ in and among you, the hope and guarantee of [realizing the] glory" (Colossians 1:27 AMP).*

Remember that a desire fulfilled is a tree of life and consider what God's desire is for his children. Jesus said it was the Father's desire to give us the kingdom:

> *"But [strive for and actively] seek His kingdom, and these things will be given to you as well. Do not be afraid and anxious, little flock, for it is your Father's good pleasure to give you the kingdom. Sell your possessions (show compassion) and give [donations] to the poor. Provide money belts for yourselves that do not wear out, an unfailing and inexhaustible treasure in the heavens, where no thief comes near and no moth destroys. For where your treasure is, there your heart will be also'" (Luke 12:31-34 AMP).*

> *"Then the kingdom and the dominion and the greatness of all the kingdoms under the whole heaven will be given to the people of the saints (believers) of the Most High; His kingdom will be an everlasting kingdom, and all the dominions will serve and obey Him" (Daniel 7:27 AMP).*

♫ **Pause and listen to *End of the Age: Book Three, "Take Possession."*** ♫

Precept 6: The River within the City

Once we understand that the prophet Jeremiah was called a city, a pillar, and bronze walls as well as the fact that Jesus likened his disciples to a city on a hill, then the mystery begins to become even clearer. We are his holy city, fashioned of living stones, the Bride of Christ, coming down as a cloud and revealed from heaven in the earth with the purpose of convincing the world that Jesus was sent by God and to inherit the seats of judgment in the earth. We are called to serve the needy, the poor, the orphans, the widows...and ultimately to rebuke and judge the wicked and bring everything under our Savior's dominion, under his feet.

"For Christ must reign [as King] until He has put all His enemies under His feet" (1 Corinthians 15:25 AMP).

He subdues His enemies under Him, those who reject Him openly.

"And then I saw thrones, and sitting on them were those to whom judgment [that is, the authority to act as judges] was given. And I saw the souls of those who had been beheaded because of their testimony of Jesus and because of the word of God, and those who had refused to worship the beast or his image, and had not accepted his mark on their forehead and on their hand; and they came to life and reigned with Christ for a thousand years" (Revelation 20:4 AMP).

We will return to the idea of where the wicked must be confronted when we address the topic of the city gate. Now let us turn our attention to the river within the city.

The Rivers of Living Water and the Knowledge of God

> *"in the middle of its street. On either side of the river was the tree of life, bearing twelve kinds of fruit, yielding its fruit every month; and the leaves of the tree were for the healing of the nations" (Revelation 22:2 AMP).*

> *"But [the time is coming when] the earth shall be filled With the knowledge of the glory of the Lord, As the waters cover the sea" (Habakkuk 2:14 AMP)."*

> *"'He who believes in Me [who adheres to, trusts in, and relies on Me], as the Scripture has said, 'From his innermost being will flow continually rivers of living water'" (John 7:38 AMP).*

Are you getting the picture? Rivers. Waters. They fill the earth with the knowledge of God.

And what is this river of life anyway? What did Jesus teach the woman at the well about natural water and living spiritual water?

> *"Jesus answered her, 'If you knew [about] God's gift [of eternal life], and who it is who says, 'Give Me a drink,' you would have asked Him [instead], and He would have given you living water (eternal life).' She said to Him, 'Sir, You have nothing to draw with [no bucket and rope] and the well is deep. Where then do You get that living water? Are You greater than our father Jacob, who gave us the well, and who used to drink from it himself, and his sons and his cattle also?' Jesus answered her, 'Everyone who drinks this water will be thirsty again. But whoever drinks the water that I give him will never be thirsty again. **But the water that I give him will become in him a spring of water [satisfying his thirst for God] welling up [continually flowing, bubbling within him] to eternal life"** (John*

4:10-14 AMP).

"But his delight is in the law of the Lord, And on His law [His precepts and teachings] he [habitually] meditates day and night. And he will be like a tree firmly planted [and fed] by streams of water, Which yields its fruit in its season; Its leaf does not wither; And in whatever he does, he prospers [and comes to maturity]. The wicked [those who live in disobedience to God's law] are not so, But they are like the chaff [worthless and without substance] which the wind blows away. Therefore the wicked will not stand [unpunished] in the judgment, Nor sinners in the assembly of the righteous. For the Lord knows and fully approves the way of the righteous, But the way of the wicked shall perish" (Psalm 1:2-6 AMP).

The river of life is the gift of eternal spiritual life available only by and through Jesus Christ. Just as he said. All we have to do is repent from sin, believe in Jesus and ask Him to fill us with the water of life that only He can give.

Jesus, the Living Word of God

"Jesus said to him, 'I am the [only] Way [to God] and the [real] Truth and the [real] Life; no one comes to the Father but through Me'" (John 14:6 AMP).

"In the beginning [before all time] was the Word (Christ), and the Word was with God, and the Word was God Himself. He was [continually existing] in the beginning [coeternally] with God. All things were made and came into existence through Him; and without Him not even one thing was made that has come into being. In Him was life [and the power to bestow life], and the life was the Light of men. The Light shines on in the darkness, and the darkness did not understand it or overpower it or appropriate it or absorb it [and is unreceptive to it]" (John 1:15 AMP).

"He is the exact living image [the essential manifestation] of the unseen God [the visible representation of the invisible], the firstborn [the preeminent one, the sovereign, and the originator] of all creation. For by Him all things were

created in heaven and on earth, [things] visible and invisible, whether thrones or dominions or rulers or authorities; all things were created and exist through Him [that is, by His activity] and for Him. And He Himself existed and is before all things, and in Him all things hold together. [His is the controlling, cohesive force of the universe.] He is also the head [the lifesource and leader] of the body, the church; and He is the beginning, the firstborn from the dead, so that He Himself will occupy the first place [He will stand supreme and be preeminent] in everything. For it pleased the Father for all the fullness [of deity—the sum total of His essence, all His perfection, powers, and attributes] to dwell [permanently] in Him (the Son), and through [the intervention of] the Son to reconcile all things to Himself, making peace [with believers] through the blood of His cross; through Him, [I say,] whether things on earth or things in heaven" (Colossians 1:15-20 AMP).

Precept 7: Consider the gates, the wicked courts and judges in the land

♫ Pause and listen to *End of the Age: Book One, "Kingdom Trumpet."*
Also pause and listen to *End of the Age: Book Two, "Leave the Temple."* ♫

In the Old Testament, the king or appointed judges would sit in the city gate and decide arguments and legal matters between the people of the city. The city gate refers the place where laws and judgment and/or execution was passed to decide a given case, lawsuit or crime. Today it would refer to the enforcement of the laws of the land, some of which are currently considered to be ones that call evil good. Consider the following:

> *"You love evil more than good, And falsehood more than speaking what is right. Selah" (Psalm 52:3 AMP).*

> *"Rebelling against and denying the Lord, Turning away from [following] our God, Speaking oppression and revolt, Conceiving and muttering from the heart lying words. Justice is pushed back, And righteous behavior stands far away; For truth has fallen in the city square, And integrity cannot enter. Yes, truth is missing;* ***And he who turns away from evil makes himself a prey****. Now the Lord saw it,* ***And it displeased Him that there was no justice"*** *(Isaiah 59:13-15 AMP).*

41

Some of you may say that these are old scriptures that have no bearing on our present history or condition. Please reconsider:

> *"The grass withers, the flower fades, But the word of our God stands forever" (Isaiah 40:8 AMP).*

There are scriptures, just like the one from Isaiah above, scattered all throughout the Bible about the wickedness that did arise in the city gate and that does arise in the city gate in this last day. The words and judgments are timeless, because Truth does not change. God desires justice in the city gate, wherever that is and at whatever level in government that may be.

The elders of the city sat in the gate where court was held

> *"then his father and mother shall take hold of him, and bring him out to the elders of his city at the gateway of his hometown" (Deuteronomy 21:19 AMP).*

> *"He would get up early and stand beside the road to the gate [of the city, where court was held]; and when any man who had a dispute came to the king for judgment, Absalom would call to him, 'From what city are you?' And he would say, 'Your servant is from one of the tribes of Israel'" (2 Samuel 15:2 AMP).*

This use of "city gate(s)" or "gateway to the city" in the Old Testament gives new meaning, perhaps, to the following verse. The juxtaposition of the phrase "gates of hell" with keys (authority) to the "kingdom of heaven" possibly call for a legal application of the verses:

> *"Then Jesus answered him, 'Blessed [happy, spiritually secure, favored by God] are you, Simon son of Jonah, because flesh and blood (mortal man) did not reveal this to you, but My Father who is in heaven. And I say to you that you are Peter, and on this rock I will build My church; and the gates of Hades (death) will not overpower it [by preventing the resurrection of the Christ]. I will give you the*

*keys (authority) of the kingdom of heaven; and whatever
you bind [forbid, declare to be improper and unlawful]
on earth will have [already] been bound in heaven, and
whatever you loose [permit, declare lawful] on earth will
have [already] been loosed in heaven"* (Matthew 16:1719
AMP).

The testimony of the saint and martyrs still speaks. The words of Moses,
God's promise to Abraham, the Psalms of David and the words of the
prophets and apostles still speak. Their words and deeds judge the world
as well along with the thousands of saints who inherit the kingdom with
their living written testimony. "Behold, he comes with clouds—myriads—of saints." All of our testimonies together with the Word of God
will win the arguments in the court of law as spoken by the prophet
Daniel and the apostle John.

*"The Angel of the Lord called to Abraham from heaven a
second time and said, 'By Myself (on the basis of Who I
Am) I have sworn [an oath], declares the Lord, that since
you have done this thing and have not withheld [from Me]
your son, your only son [of promise], indeed I will greatly
bless you, and I will greatly multiply your descendants like
the stars of the heavens and like the sand on the seashore;
and **your seed shall possess the gate of their enemies
[as conquerors]. Through your seed all the nations
of the earth shall be blessed, because you have heard
and obeyed My voice**"* (Genesis 22:15-18 AMP).

Blessing comes through godly justice in the city gate.

*"But the court [of the Most High] will sit in judgment,
and his dominion will be taken away, [first to be] consumed
[gradually] and [then] to be destroyed forever. Then the
kingdom and the dominion and the greatness of all the
kingdoms under the whole heaven will be given to the people
of the saints (believers) of the Most High; His kingdom will
be an everlasting kingdom, and all the dominions will serve
and obey Him.' 'This is the end of the matter. As for me,
Daniel, my [waking] thoughts were extremely troubling*

and alarming and my face grew pale; but I kept the matter [of the vision and the angel's explanation] to myself.'" *(Daniel 7:26-28 AMP).*

*"That which is has already been, and that which will be has already been, for God seeks what has passed by [so that history repeats itself]. Moreover, I have seen under the sun that **in the place of justice there is wickedness, and in the place of righteousness there is wickedness.** I said to myself, '**God will judge both the righteous and the wicked,' for there is a time [appointed] for every matter and for every deed**" (Ecclesiastes 3:15-17 AMP).*

Precept 8: The Beatitudes and the Sermon on the Mount: You are the light of the world

We are called to make and maintain peace (blessed are the peacemakers). This is done at all levels in the city gate and places of judgment, in the courts of the land.

> *"'And He will judge between the nations, And will mediate [disputes] for many peoples; And they will beat their swords into plowshares and their spears into pruning hooks. Nation will not lift up the sword against nation, And never again will they learn war'" (Isaiah 2:4 AMP).*

We are Christ's Body

To summarize, we are Christ's body in the earth and the time for us to judge the wicked soon approaches.

> *"For no one ever hated his own body, but [instead] he nourishes and protects and cherishes it, just as Christ does the church, because we are members (parts) of His body" (Ephesians 5:29-30 AMP).*

His life is in the blood of the new covenant

And in the same way He took the cup after they had eaten, saying, "This cup, which is poured out for you, is the new covenant [ratified] in My blood" (Luke 22:20 AMP).

"And they overcame and conquered him because of the blood of the Lamb and because of the word of their testimony, for they did not love their life and renounce their faith even when faced with death" (Revelation 12:11 AMP).

"And then I saw thrones, and sitting on them were those to whom judgment [that is, the authority to act as judges] was given. And I saw the souls of those who had been beheaded because of their testimony of Jesus and because of the word of God, and those who had refused to worship the beast or his image, and had not accepted his mark on their forehead and on their hand; and they came to life and reigned with Christ for a thousand years" (Revelation 20:4 AMP).

As for Revelation 20:4 and the phrase "came to life" above, it may signify that the saints are invigorated and stand to their feet to inherit the kingdom with new life. I also understand that in the Hebrew wedding the bride and groom are seated on chairs and lifted up and paraded around the room. During the time of renewal spoken of by Jesus, that would correspond to the lifting up and celebration of Jesus Christ and his Bride, the Church. Perhaps this refers to moving from a place of marginalization and being the prey of the wicked, to being seated on chairs (thrones) and celebrated. This is what we are looking forward to. I am reminded of the Lord's Prayer and the portion, "thy will be done in earth as it is in heaven." The saints who have gone before reign, then, from heaven through their testimony as recorded in history, and the saints in the earth reign through the inheritance of the promise of the kingdom—the mystery spoken of by the prophets and revealed in Revelation at the proper time. Just as there are books that are opened and revealed to our understanding here, perhaps there are books in heaven that are opened when the day of judgment begins. "Thy will be done in earth as it is in heaven."

We see portions dimly

I am only sharing with you that which the Spirit has taught me and brought to my remembrance. For we see in part and we see darkly as through a glass sometimes. If the saints come to life and reign with Christ, is it their literal body or is it the fact that their testimony is ultimately vindicated and rises from the dust to judge the world along with the Word of God and those of us who remain? Maybe it means they are ushered into the life of the kingdom inheritance in a physical resurrection. I do not know. One thing I do know for certain: the righteous possess the gates in the kingdom and execute judgement on the wicked. We are responsible for what God does reveal to us. If it is time for us to act, then we must act.

"For now [in this time of imperfection] we see in a mirror dimly [a blurred reflection, a riddle, an enigma], but then [when the time of perfection comes we will see reality] face to face. Now I know in part [just in fragments], but then I will know fully, just as I have been fully known [by God]" (1 Corinthians 13:12 AMP).

Precept 9: The Bookends of Kingdom Inheritance

♫ Pause and listen to *End of the Age: Book One, "Abraham's Children."* ♫

Bookend 1: The promised kingdom victory in Genesis chapter 3

> *"The Lord God said to the serpent, 'Because you have done this, You are cursed more than all the cattle, And more than any animal of the field; On your belly you shall go, And dust you shall eat All the days of your life. And I will put enmity (open hostility) Between you and the woman, And between your seed (offspring) and her [Seed; He shall [fatally] bruise your head, And you shall [only] bruise His heel.'"(Genesis 3:14-15 AMP).*

The reference here to a coming "seed" is to the seed of the woman. Women do not bear the seed for offspring, men do. This is a prophecy of the virgin birth in Genesis chapter three. The serpent will bruise the Messiah's heel—a wound not unto death—and the messiah will fatally bruise the serpent's head and defeat him. In Genesis 22 we find the next part of that promise:

> *"The Angel of the Lord called to Abraham from heaven a second time and said, 'By Myself (on the basis of Who I Am) I have sworn [an oath], declares the Lord, that since you have done this thing and have not withheld [from Me]*

your son, your only son [of promise], indeed I will greatly bless you, and I will greatly multiply your descendants like the stars of the heavens and like the sand on the seashore; and your seed shall possess the gate of their enemies [as conquerors]. Through your seed all the nations of the earth shall be blessed, because you have heard and obeyed My voice" (Genesis 22:15-18 AMP).

Inheritance of the saints

"[we pray that you may be] strengthened and invigorated with all power, according to His glorious might, to attain every kind of endurance and patience with joy; giving thanks to the Father, who has qualified us to share in the **inheritance** of the saints (God's people) in the Light" (Colossians 1:11-13 AMP).

This is our current spiritual position in heaven. The inheritance in the earth is all about timing. It occurs in the earth as what we were taught to pray is ultimately fulfilled:

"So He said to them, 'When you pray, say: Our Father in heaven, Hallowed be Your name. Your kingdom come. Your will be done On earth as it is in heaven'" (Luke 11: 2 NKJV).)

His will on earth will not occur without the unity of the body of Christ and the "possession of the city gates" by the saints.

Bookend 2: The Eternal Kingdom

♫ Pause and listen to *End of the Age: Book Three, "Take Possession."* ♫

"'But the saints (believers) of the Most High [God] will receive the kingdom and possess the kingdom forever, for all ages to come.' " (Daniel 7:18 AMP).

"until the Ancient of Days came and judgment was passed in favor of the saints of the Most High [God], and the time arrived when the saints (believers) took possession of the kingdom" (Daniel 7:22 AMP).

"'Then the kingdom and the dominion and the greatness of all the kingdoms under the whole heaven will be given to the people of the saints (believers) of the Most High; His kingdom will be an everlasting kingdom, and all the dominions will serve and obey Him'" (Daniel 7:27 AMP).

"And then I saw thrones, and sitting on them were those to whom judgment [that is, the authority to act as judges] was given. And I saw the souls of those who had been beheaded because of their testimony of Jesus and because of the word of God, and those who had refused to worship the beast or his image, and had not accepted his mark on their forehead and on their hand; and they came to life and reigned with Christ for a thousand years" (Revelation 20:4 AMP).

Thrones. Plural. Saints, beaten and trodden down by the wicked and silenced through the generations. Many tortured and put to death. Martyred. Yet their testimony rises from the dust to speak and vindicate their faith on the day of judgment. The saints are finally given their rightful place of authority which they carry out through the power of God's Word, their testimony and Christ's redemptive work. It is God's legacy gift to us to redeem mankind and to redeem the earth and bring all things under the feet of Jesus Christ.

Precept 10: The Saviors of Obadiah and Jesus

♫ Pause and listen to *End of the Age: Book One, "Kingdom Trumpet."* ♫

> *"And He will send His angels with a loud trumpet and they will gather together His elect (God's chosen ones) from the four winds, from one end of the heavens to the other"* *(Matthew 24:31 AMP).*

Consider that the "angels," mentioned above, and "deliverers," mentioned below, carry forth the message of the revealed kingdom judgments. The riddle, as Jesus did speak in riddles and parables, is this: Jesus sends out His servants, chosen saints, to do His bidding and to take the wicked from their places of authority and judge them with the Word, the fire and Sword of His mouth (see Precept 11).

> *"The deliverers shall go up on Mount Zion To rule and judge the mountain of Esau, And the kingdom and the kingship shall be the Lord's"* *(Obadiah 1:21 AMP).*

If you know the story of Esau, you know that he valued the appetites of the flesh more than the blessing and promise of God. We must consider this when interpreting this verse. At this time the plowman overtakes the harvesters.

"'Behold, the days are coming,' says the Lord, 'When the plowman shall overtake the one who gathers the harvest, And the one who treads the grapes [shall overtake] him who sows the seed [for the harvest continues until planting time]; When the mountains will drip sweet wine And all the hills shall melt [that is, everything that was once barren will overflow with streams of blessing]'" (Amos 9:13 AMP).

Precept 11: The Kingdom Laws of the Sword, Hammer and Rod

♫ Pause and listen to *End of the Age: Book One, "Jesus' Sword."* ♫

The Sword of the Spirit is the Word of God

> *"And take the helmet of salvation, and the sword of the Spirit, which is the Word of God" (Ephesians 6:17 AMP).*

> *"For the word of God is living and active and full of power [making it operative, energizing, and effective]. It is sharper than any twoedged sword, penetrating as far as the division of the soul and spirit [the completeness of a person], and of both joints and marrow [the deepest parts of our nature], exposing and judging the very thoughts and intentions of the heart" (Hebrews 4:12 AMP).*

The **word of God** is considered the **sword of His mouth** in Revelation. It is used to judge. Note that it is not man's word that is used to judge. Only God's word is used to judge. This is an important point that needs to be understood.

> *"In His right hand He held seven stars, and from His mouth came a sharp twoedged sword [of judgment]; and His face [reflecting His majesty and the Shekinah glory] was like the sun shining in [all] its power [at midday]" (Revelation*

1:16 AMP).

In Genesis and Daniel, the descendants of Abraham and the saints of the Most High are compared to stars.

> *"Therefore repent [change your inner self—your old way of thinking, your sinful behavior—seek God's will]; or else I am coming to you quickly, and I will make war and fight against them with the sword of My mouth [in judgment]"* (Revelation 2:16 AMP).

> *"If anyone is destined for captivity, he will go into captivity; if anyone kills with a sword, he must be killed with a sword. Here is [the call for] the patient endurance and the faithfulness of the saints [which is seen in the response of God's people to difficult times]"* (Revelation 13:10 AMP).

> *"From His mouth comes a sharp sword (His word) with which He may strike down the nations, and He will rule them with a rod of iron; and He will tread the wine press of the fierce wrath of God, the Almighty [in judgment of the rebellious world]"* (Revelation 19:15 AMP).

> *"He who withholds the rod [of discipline] hates his son, But he who loves him disciplines and trains him diligently and appropriately [with wisdom and love] (Proverbs 13:24 AMP).*

The rod of discipline is used in love. The sword and fire is used for judgment.

God's Word is also like a fire and a hammer. I repeat, man's word cannot accomplish this. It must be God's word.

> *"Is not My word like fire [that consumes all that cannot endure the test]?' says the LORD, 'and like a hammer that breaks the [most stubborn] rock [in pieces]?'"* (Jeremiah 23:29 AMP).

> *"And the nations (Gentiles) became enraged, and Your*

wrath and indignation came, and the time came for the dead to be judged, and [the time came] to reward Your bondservants the prophets and the saints (God's people) and those who fear Your name, the small and the great, and [the time came] to destroy the destroyers of the earth" (Revelation 11:18 AMP).

"See to it that you do not refuse [to listen to] Him who is speaking [to you now]. For if those [sons of Israel] did not escape when they refused [to listen to] him who warned them on earth [revealing God's will], how much less will we escape if we turn our backs on Him who warns from heaven? His voice shook the earth [at Mount Sinai] then, but now He has given a promise, saying, 'Yet once more I will shake not only the earth, but also the [starry] heaven.' Now this [expression], 'Yet once more,' indicates the removal and final transformation of all those things which can be shaken—that is, of that which has been created—so that those things which cannot be shaken may remain" (Hebrews 12:25-27 AMP).

You, the saints in Christ, the Body of Christ, His Body, and He is the Head, will judge the world. This cannot be done sitting in the pew or staring at the sky waiting to be rescued. It will happen when every saint worth his or her salt (Matthew 5:3) takes up the armor of God of Ephesians 6 and publishes the word of God concerning the wicked to every corner of the earth.

Precept 12: Courtroom testimony and opening of the books

♫ Pause and listen to *End of the Age: Book Two, "Leave the Temple."* ♫

The phrase *book of life* occurs 8 times in the Holy Scriptures: Psalm 69:28; Philippians 4:3; Revelation 3:5; 13:8; 17:8; 20:12; 20:15; 21:27.

> *"And I saw the dead, the great and the small, standing before the throne, and books were opened. Then another book was opened, which is the Book of Life; and the dead were judged according to what they had done as written in the books [that is, everything done while on earth]" (Revelation 20:12 AMP).*

The book of life in heaven contains all the works of the dead during their lives in the earth. Interestingly, the Books of Moses, the prophets, and the apostles contain the works of the wicked and spiritually dead here in the earth as well. Hence, the "books" were opened. "Opened" can also refer to "opening to our understanding and secrets revealed" as mentioned previously. Consider the following:

> *"The entire vision [of all these things] will be to you like the words of a scroll that is sealed, which they give to one who*

59

can read, saying, 'Read this, please,' he shall say, 'I cannot, for it is sealed'" (Isaiah 29:11 AMP).

"But as for you, Daniel, conceal these words and seal up the scroll until the end of time. Many will go back and forth and search anxiously [through the scroll], and knowledge [of the purpose of God as revealed by His prophets] will [greatly] increase" (Daniel 12:4 AMP).

"A river of fire was flowing And coming out from before Him; Thousands upon thousands were serving Him, And myriads upon myriads were standing before Him; The court convened, And the books were opened" (Daniel 7:10 AMP).

This does not speak of a literal river of fire. Consider again the parallel pages of the Word of God and fire and the different ways to interpret scripture. The river of fire is the "river" of the Word of God in judgment that flows before him. The "opening of the books" means that the secrets are revealed from heaven to our understanding. There is no more waiting to understand for we will all understand. Interestingly enough, all the works of the wicked and the righteous are already listed in the books that we have right now, from Genesis to Revelation. When the secrets of the books are opened the following verses are fulfilled:

"'And each man will no longer teach his neighbor and his brother, saying, 'Know the Lord,' for they will all know Me [through personal experience], from the least of them to the greatest,' says the Lord. 'For I will forgive their wickedness, and I will no longer remember their sin'" (Jeremiah 31:34 AMP).

"But [the time is coming when] the earth shall be filled With the knowledge of the glory of the Lord, As the waters cover the sea" (Habakkuk 2:14 AMP).

HARVEST OF THOSE WHO BELIEVE

Precept 13: The spiritual children of Abraham shine forth

♬ Pause and listen to *End of the Age: Book Two, "I See the Clouds."* ♬

"Those who are [spiritually] wise will shine brightly like the brightness of the expanse of heaven, and those who lead many to righteousness, [will shine] like the stars forever and ever" (Daniel 12:3 AMP).

"Blessed [spiritually calm with life-joy in God's favor] are the makers and maintainers of peace, for they will [express His character and] be called the sons of God" (Matthew 5:9 AMP).

"And He will judge between the nations, And will mediate [disputes] for many peoples; And they will beat their swords into plowshares and their spears into pruning hooks. Nation will not lift up the sword against nation, And never again will they learn war" (Isaiah 2:4 AMP).

"So He who was sitting on the cloud cast His sickle over the earth, and the earth was reaped (judged)" (Revelation 14:16 AMP).

"each one's work will be clearly shown [for what it is]; for the

63

day [of judgment] will disclose it, because it is to be revealed with fire, and the fire will test the quality and character and worth of each person's work" (1 Corinthians 3:13 AMP).

Remember, the workers are the angels, God's servants. The fire and hammer is the word that tests the works of men. The unity of the body is required for harvest.

Precept 14: The Mind of the Flesh and the Judgment

> *"Now the mind of the flesh is death [both now and forever—because it pursues sin]; but the mind of the Spirit is life and peace [the spiritual wellbeing that comes from walking with God—both now and forever]; the mind of the flesh [with its sinful pursuits] is actively hostile to God. It does not submit itself to God's law, since it cannot, and those who are in the flesh [living a life that caters to sinful appetites and impulses] cannot please God" (Romans 8:6-8 AMP).*

The last days before the renewal will be very difficult and dangerous

> *"But understand this, that in the last days dangerous times [of great stress and trouble] will come [difficult days that will be hard to bear]. For people will be lovers of self [narcissistic, self-focused], lovers of money [impelled by greed], boastful, arrogant, revilers, disobedient to parents, ungrateful, unholy and profane, [and they will be] unloving [devoid of natural human affection, calloused and inhumane], irreconcilable, malicious gossips, devoid of self-control [intemperate, immoral], brutal, haters of good, traitors, reckless, conceited, lovers of [sensual] pleasure rather than lovers of God, holding to a form of [outward] godliness (religion), although they have denied its power [for their*

65

conduct nullifies their claim of faith]. Avoid such people and keep far away from them. For among them are those who worm their way into homes and captivate morally weak and spiritually dwarfed women weighed down by [the burden of their] sins, easily swayed by various impulses, always learning and listening to anybody who will teach them, but never able to come to the knowledge of the truth. Just as Jannes and Jambres [the court magicians of Egypt] opposed Moses, so these men also oppose the truth, men of depraved mind, unqualified and worthless [as teachers] in regard to the faith. But they will not get very far, for their meaningless nonsense and ignorance will become obvious to everyone, as was that of Jannes and Jambres" (2 Timothy 3:1-9 AMP).

At a specific time, God gathers His saints for the purpose of judgment

"It was about these people that Enoch, in the seventh generation from Adam, prophesied, when he said, 'Look, the Lord came with myriads of His holy ones to execute judgment upon all, and to convict all the ungodly of all the ungodly deeds they have done in an ungodly way, and of all the harsh and cruel things ungodly sinners have spoken against Him.' These people are [habitual] murmurers, griping and complaining, following after their own desires [controlled by passion]; they speak arrogantly, [pretending admiration and] flattering people to gain an advantage. But as for you, beloved, remember the [prophetic] words spoken by the apostles of our Lord Jesus Christ. They used to say to you, 'In the last days there will be scoffers, following after their own ungodly passions.' These are the ones who are [agitators] causing divisions—worldly minded [secular, unspiritual, carnal, merely sensual—unsaved], devoid of the Spirit. But you, beloved, build yourselves up on [the foundation of] your most holy faith [continually progress, rise like an edifice higher and higher], pray in the Holy Spirit, and keep yourselves in the love of God, waiting anxiously and looking forward to the mercy of our Lord Jesus Christ [which will bring you] to eternal life. And have mercy on some, who are doubting; save others, snatching them out of the fire; and on some have mercy but with fear, loathing even the clothing spotted and polluted by their shameless immoral freedom.

Now to Him who is able to keep you from stumbling or falling into sin, and to present you unblemished [blameless and faultless] in the presence of His glory with triumphant joy and unspeakable delight, to the only God our Savior, through Jesus Christ our Lord, be glory, majesty, dominion, and power, before all time and now and forever. Amen" (Jude 1:1425 AMP).

"In fact, so terrifying was the sight, that Moses said, 'I am filled with fear and trembling.' But you have come to Mount Zion and to the city of the living God, the heavenly Jerusalem, and to myriads of angels [in festive gathering], and to the general assembly and assembly of the firstborn who are registered [as citizens] in heaven, and to God, who is Judge of all, and to the spirits of the righteous (the redeemed in heaven) who have been made perfect [bringing them to their final glory]" (Hebrews 12:21-23 AMP).

As was discussed before, we are God's holy city of living stones, the mountain of his house, bearing his Spirit in earthly vessels that the glory might be his own.

"But we have this precious treasure [the good news about salvation] in [unworthy] earthen vessels [of human frailty], so that the grandeur and surpassing greatness of the power will be [shown to be] from God [His sufficiency] and not from ourselves" (2 Corinthians 4:7 AMP).

The wicked will be judged. Their nonsense and foolishness will be evident to all when the books are opened and the works of the wicked are revealed by the consuming fire of the Word of God.

"each one's work will be clearly shown [for what it is]; for the day [of judgment] will disclose it, because it is to be revealed with fire, and the fire will test the quality and character and worth of each person's work" (1 Corinthians 3:13 AMP).

The value of spiritual wisdom

This keeping of secrets is even addressed in the teachings of Jesus. Those that value spiritual wisdom and are receptive to God's word will understand and be given more wisdom.

"For whoever has [spiritual wisdom because he is receptive to God's word], to him more will be given, and he will be richly and abundantly supplied; but whoever does not have [spiritual wisdom because he has devalued God's word], even what he has will be taken away from him. This is the reason I speak to the crowds in parables: because while [having the power of] seeing they do not see, and while [having the power of] hearing they do not hear, nor do they understand and grasp [spiritual things]. In them the prophecy of Isaiah is being fulfilled, which says, 'You will hear and keep on hearing, but never understand; And you will look and keep on looking, but never comprehend'" (Matthew 13:12-14 AMP).

"Let the sea roar, and all the things that fill it; Let the field rejoice, and all that is in it. Then the trees of the forest will sing for joy before the Lord; For He comes to judge and govern the earth. O give thanks to the Lord, for He is good; For His lovingkindness endures forever" (1 Chronicles 16:32-34 AMP).

He put a new song in my mouth, a song of praise to our God; Many will see and fear [with great reverence] And will trust confidently in the Lord" (Psalm 40:3 AMP).

And they sang a new song [of glorious redemption], saying, 'Worthy and deserving are You to take the scroll and to break its seals; for You were slain (sacrificed), and with Your blood You purchased people for God from every tribe and language and people and nation'" (Revelation 5:9 AMP).

"Then I saw another mighty angel coming down from heaven, clothed in a cloud, with a rainbow (halo) over his head; and his face was like the sun, and his feet (legs) were like columns of fire; and he had a little book (scroll) open in his hand. He set his right foot on the sea and his left foot on the land; and he shouted with a loud voice, like the roaring

of a lion [compelling attention and inspiring awe]; and when he had shouted out, the seven peals of thunder spoke with their own voices [uttering their message in distinct words]. And when the seven peals of thunder had spoken, I was about to write; but I heard a voice from heaven saying, "'Seal up the things which the seven peals of thunder have spoken and do not write them down." Then the angel whom I had seen standing on the sea and the land raised his right hand [to swear an oath] to heaven, and swore [an oath] by [the name of] Him who lives forever and ever, who created heaven and the things in it, and the earth and the things in it, and the sea and the things in it, that there will be delay no longer, but when it is time for the trumpet call of the seventh angel, when he is about to sound, then the mystery of God [that is, His hidden purpose and plan] is finished, as He announced the gospel to His servants the prophets'" (Revelation 10:1-7 AMP).

The Hidden Mystery and Inheritance of the Saints

As we have seen in our riddle, "angels" can refer to sons of God or servants of God, that is, the saints. We can interpret some of the descriptive language here. The halo represents a crown. The servant's legs are flames of fire because he receives all of his strength from the Word of God. The little scroll is "open" because it reveals the hidden purpose and plan of God as announced in the Books of Moses, the prophets and the apostles. His face is like the sun because he constantly is beholden to the Word of God. So what is the finishing of the mystery of God spoken of by the prophets? To inherit judgment. Again I repeat: the judgment are the words written in the Word, not man's words.

"To execute on them the judgment written. This is the honor for all His godly ones. Praise the Lord! (Hallelujah!)" (Psalm 149:9 AMP).

"Do you not know that the saints (God's people) will [one day] judge the world? If the world is to be judged by you, are you not competent to try trivial (insignificant, petty) cases?" (1 Corinthians 6:2 AMP).

Precept 15: Harvest Season, the Parable of the Sower, and other scriptures

The **seed is the Word** of God.

> "Now [the meaning of] the parable is this: **The seed is the word of God [concerning eternal salvation]**. Those beside the road are the people who have heard; then the devil comes and takes the message [of God] away from their hearts, so that they will not believe [in Me as the Messiah] and be saved" (Luke 8:11-12 AMP).

> "Jesus gave them another parable [to consider], saying, 'The kingdom of heaven is like a man who sowed good seed in his field. But while his men were sleeping, his enemy came and sowed weeds [resembling wheat] among the wheat, and went away. So when the plants sprouted and formed grain, the weeds appeared also. The servants of the owner came to him and said, 'Sir, did you not sow good seed in your field? Then how does it have weeds in it?' He replied to them, 'An enemy has done this.' The servants asked him, 'Then do you want us to go and pull them out?' But he said, 'No; because as you pull out the weeds, you may uproot the wheat with them. Let them grow together until the harvest; and at harvest time I will tell the reapers, "First gather the weeds and tie them in bundles to be burned; but gather the wheat into my barn"'" (Matthew 13:24-30 AMP).

71

Harvest season is about gathering wheat into the barn. There is good wheat and even bad weeds—resembling the good wheat no less are gathered and separated.

*"and the enemy who sowed them is the devil, and the harvest is the **end of the age**; and the reapers are angels. So just as the weeds are gathered up and burned in the fire, so will it be at the end of the age. The Son of Man will send out His angels, and they will gather out of His kingdom **all things that offend [those things by which people are let into sin]**, and will throw them into the furnace of fire; in that place there will be weeping [over sorrow and pain] and grinding of teeth [over distress and anger]. Then the righteous [those that seek the will of God] will shine forth [radiating the new life] like the sun in the kingdom of their Father. He who has ears [to hear], let him hear and heed My words" (Matthew 13:39-43 AMP).*

Paul defined for the Galatians what the fruit of the flesh was as well as the fruit of the Spirit: the fruit of the flesh is sexual immorality, impurity, indecent behavior, idolatry, witchcraft, hostilities, strife, jealousy, outbursts of anger, selfish ambition, dissensions, factions, envy, drunkenness, carousing, and things like these; the fruit of the Spirit includes love, joy, peace, patience, kindness, goodness, faithfulness, gentleness, self-control (Galatians 5:19-23). Moses and the prophets taught us the difference between good fruit and bad fruit, wickedness and righteousness, justice and injustice, ruling with mercy and without mercy. One of the bad fruits in the Old Testament was the receiving of bribes. Now, you should be catching on by now that everything needed for harvest and judgment has been made available to us. The weeds are to be separated first and tied off. The wicked must be named. Then gather the wheat into the barn for protection and the wedding supper.

So, pray. Find your place. Form ranks. Prepare for action. Pray for wisdom. Seek counsel. The books are opening. Tie up your arguments with words from the books regarding the wicked, the rich, the rebellious, the non-believing and those who practice witchcraft. Jesus is the Word of God revealed in the Gospel of John chapter one. His book, his Word, his Body the Church, his testimony, our testimony, his blood, Moses and the prophets looking forward to the cross and we looking back at the cross—it is all part of the opening the books. All of it is about giving glory to God, Jehovah, the Most High God who redeems us from the pit of eternal separation from Him through the gift of His son (Isaiah 53). His ways are unsearchable and past finding out. For God's ways are higher than our ways. His love is...boundless. This is his legacy, His kingdom promise. This is our inheritance to pass on to our children and to our children's children both now and forever.

> "He has made everything beautiful and appropriate in its time. He has also planted eternity [a sense of divine purpose] in the human heart [a mysterious longing which nothing under the sun can satisfy, except God]—yet man cannot find out (comprehend, grasp) what God has done (His overall plan) from the beginning to the end" (Ecclesiastes 3:11 AMP).

Behold, He stands at the door and knocks. Will you open the door? Do not harden your heart and reject him. If you do you will be left outside during the wedding feast and the door will remain shut and you will not enter. Outside will be wailing and gnashing of teeth for your opportunity will be gone. Inside the meek and pure of heart will feast on the vindication of their faith and banquet of kingdom promises fulfilled. They will partake of the Lord's Supper and rejoice. They will celebrate the body and blood of Jesus Christ, the Lamb slain before the foundation of the world. They will sing with joy. We will go out on that day like those that dream (Psalm 126). We will sow and reap on the same day (Amos 9:13). We will burst forth from the stall and skip about and trample the wicked (Malachi 4:13). Oh what a glorious day that will be when the saints go marching in. If you cannot stand in the gate because you are bedridden sick or in the hospital, sing praise to God and rejoice with your brothers and sisters in Christ for you got to see the day come before entering your eternal rest. If you have the strength, pass this along to someone else. If you do not, may you enter our Lord's eternal domain in peace. May His peace guard your hearts both now and forevermore. Amen.

May the grace of our Father, the fear of God and the steadfastness of the Son's obedience to the Father well up in you all, both now and forever.

Those who break the commandments and teach others to do so will be called the least in the kingdom of heaven

"So whoever breaks one of the least [important] of these commandments, and teaches others to do the same, will be called least [important] in the kingdom of heaven; but whoever practices and teaches them, he will be called great in the kingdom of heaven" (Matthew 5:19 AMP).

Praise be to our Redeemer. Christ is risen. He will bring us to unity in this hour. Pray for the peace of Jerusalem. Amen. Teach these things to your children.

Do ye still not understand? For Jesus spoke in parables. The LORD spoke in visions, dreams and riddles in the Old Testament. The saints are the living stones; they are the cloud of witnesses past and present; they are the trees of the field; they are as the angels of heaven; they are ambassadors for Christ. The workers are the "angels" and chosen servants of the kingdom that work in the field at the time of harvest. They gather the wheat into the barn and burn the weeds in the fire of God's word, for He is a consuming fire. They raise the banner; they sing the Song of Moses that spoke of the judgment that would befall the wayward in the later days.

Precept 16: The River of Fire and the Messengers of Fire

The fire of God is the Word of God that judges and refines. It is a river of life to those who fear Him and a river of the fiery judgment of His eternal Word to those in rebellion to His law.

> *"so that the genuineness of your faith, which is much more precious than gold which is perishable, even though tested and purified by fire, may be found to result in [your] praise and glory and honor at the revelation of Jesus Christ" (1 Peter 1:7).*

> *"A river of fire was flowing And coming out from before Him; A thousand thousands were attending Him, And ten thousand times ten thousand were standing before Him; The court was seated, And the books were opened" (Daniel 7:10).*

> *"Therefore, thus says the Lord God of hosts, "Because you [people] have spoken this word, Behold, I am making My words a fire in your mouth [Jeremiah] And this people wood, and My words will consume them" (Jeremiah 5:14).*

> *"And if anyone wants to harm them, fire comes out of their mouth and devours their enemies; so if anyone wants to harm them, he must be killed in this way" (Revelation 11:5).*

> *"'Is not My word like fire [that consumes all that can-*

not endure the test]?'" says the Lord, "'and like a hammer that breaks the [most stubborn] rock [in pieces]?'" (Jeremiah 23:29 AMP).

"But by His word the present heavens and earth are being reserved for fire, being kept for the day of judgment and destruction of the ungodly people" (2 Peter 3:7 AMP).

"Now look, the name of the Lord comes from far away, Burning with His anger, and heavy with smoke; His lips are full of indignation, And His tongue is like a consuming fire" (Isaiah 30:27 AMP).

"for our God is [indeed] a consuming fire" (Hebrews 12:29 AMP).

"each one's work will be clearly shown [for what it is]; for the day [of judgment] will disclose it, because it is to be revealed with fire, and the fire will test the quality and character and worth of each person's work" (1 Corinthians 3:13 AMP).

"and to give relief to you who are so distressed and to us as well when the Lord Jesus is revealed from heaven with His mighty angels in a flame of fire (2 Thessalonians 1:7 AMP).

"And concerning the angels He says, 'Who makes His angels winds, And His ministering servants flames of fire [to do His bidding]'" (Hebrews 1:7 AMP).

"There appeared to them tongues resembling fire, which were being distributed [among them], and they rested on each one of them [as each person received the Holy Spirit]" (Acts 2:3 AMP).

If the word of the gospel of Christ lives in you and you have been reborn of the Holy Spirit, then you are one of his angels. You are one of servants. You are a flame of fire when you speak the Word of Truth against the wicked, the judgment written according to Psalm 149. Only through his word can the kingdom be established. The tradition of men and religious doctrines that put religious form and dogma above the Word of God make his Word to no effect (1 Samuel 15:23; Matthew 15:5–7). Only those who put the Word first will have their full reward.

"For God did not give us a spirit of timidity or cowardice or fear, but [He has given us a spirit] of power and of love and of sound judgment and personal discipline [abilities that result in a calm, wellbalanced mind and selfcontrol]" (2 Timothy 1:7 AMP).

"that you may eat and drink at My table in My kingdom, and you will sit on thrones judging the twelve tribes of Israel" (Luke 22:30 NASB).

"for the kingdom of God is not eating and drinking, but righteousness and peace and joy in the Holy Spirit" (Romans 14:17 NASB).

What is the lake of fire but the Word of God that covers the earth? It consumes the chaff and breaks stubborn stones that do not yield to His hammer. It causes peace to come where there was no peace. He is revealed from heaven because all Truth comes down and is revealed "from above." We carry His presence within us and unite as a cloud in the earth: rain and refreshing for the weary and as fire for the wicked to burn up wicked works of rebellion. I know many of these teachings are hard for us to internalize. But "cutting time short" as Jesus said in Matthew 24:22 might just depend on us, His body and mouthpiece.

Precept 17: The Light of the World, the Stars of Heaven and the Morning Star

Jesus is the Light of the World. His followers are the light of Christ to the world.

> "Once more Jesus addressed the crowd. He said, 'I am the Light of the world. He who follows Me will not walk in the darkness, but will have the Light of life'" (John 8:12 AMP).

> "You are the light of [Christ to] the world. A city set on a hill cannot be hidden" (Matthew 5:14 AMP).

> "I have come as Light into the world, so that everyone who believes and trusts in Me [as Savior—all those who anchor their hope in Me and rely on the truth of My message] will not continue to live in darkness" (John 12:46 AMP).

> "among them the god of this world [Satan] has blinded the minds of the unbelieving to prevent them from seeing the illuminating light of the gospel of the glory of Christ, who is the image of God" (2 Corinthians 4:4 AMP).

> "so that you may prove yourselves to be blameless and guileless, innocent and uncontaminated, children of God without blemish in the midst of a [morally] crooked and [spiritually] perverted generation, among whom you are seen as

bright lights [beacons shining out clearly] in the world [of darkness]" (Philippians 2:15 AMP).

I shared the following promise before spoken to Abraham. Here we find his descendants referred to as being like the stars of the heavens:

"indeed I will greatly bless you, and I will greatly multiply your descendants like the stars of the heavens and like the sand on the seashore; and your seed shall possess the gate of their enemies [as conquerors]" (Genesis 22:17 AMP).

Daniel, Jesus and Peter all prophecy that at the end of the age the righteous would shine like the heavens:

"Those who are [spiritually] wise will shine brightly like the brightness of the expanse of heaven, and those who lead many to righteousness, [will shine] like the stars forever and ever" (Daniel 12:3 AMP).

"Then the righteous [those who seek the will of God] will shine forth [radiating the new life] like the sun in the kingdom of their Father. He who has ears [to hear], let him hear and heed My words" (Matthew 13:43 AMP).

"So we have the prophetic word made more certain. You do well to pay [close] attention to it as to a lamp shining in a dark place, until the day dawns and light breaks through the gloom and the morning star arises in your hearts" (2 Peter 1:19 AMP).

Jesus Christ is the Morning Star that rises in our hearts on the Day of the Lord.

The Morning Star

Jesus calls himself the Morning Star in Revelation 22:16. But He also says that the authority of the Morning Star is given to someone else in Revelation 2:28. This is because Jesus rules from heaven through His Word and the saints rule in the earth through the Word of Christ. This is how he taught us to pray, "Your will be done, in earth as it is in heaven."

> *"and he shall shepherd and rule them with a rod of iron, as the earthen pots are broken in pieces, as I also have received authority [and power to rule them] from My Father; and I will give him the Morning Star. He who has an ear, let him hear and heed what the Spirit says to the churches" (Revelation 2:27-29).*

The above passage from Revelation is a parallel prophecy to Psalm 2.

> *"'Yet as for Me, I have anointed and firmly installed My King Upon Zion, My holy mountain.' 'I will declare the decree of the Lord: He said to Me, 'You are My Son; This day [I proclaim] I have begotten You'" (Psalm 2:6-7 AMP).*

Jesus dwells in the mountain of his house, Mt. Zion, His body, His house made of living stones (1 Peter 2:4-5). Truth is revealed from above, to the earth through flames of fire, His ministering angels in the earth each proclaiming the Word of God as it pertains to judgment of the wicked.

> *"I kept looking Until thrones were set up, And the Ancient of Days (God) took His seat; His garment was white as snow And the hair of His head like pure wool. His throne was flames of fire; Its wheels were a burning fire. A river of fire was flowing. And coming out from before Him; A thousand thousands were attending Him, And ten thousand times ten thousand were standing before Him; The court was seated, And the books were opened" (Daniel 7:9-10).*

> *"But they shall serve the LORD their God and [the descendant of] David their King, whom I will raise up for them" (Jeremiah 30:9 AMP).*

Jesus is the Eternal King. He is the tender Branch of Jesse. The government will be on His shoulders and we take upon ourselves the yoke of the kingdom because the work has already been done. It is time to sit down at the table and partake of the kingdom promises made available to us in Christ (Isaiah 9:6; 11:1; 53:1-12).

> "I say to you that many [Gentiles] will come from east and west, and will sit down [to feast at the table, and enjoy God's promises] with Abraham, Isaac, and Jacob in the kingdom of heaven [because they accepted Me as Savior]" Matthew 8:11 AMP).

His throne is the Word of God, for He sits in judgment. Just as we saw before in Jeremiah, God's word is a consuming fire.

Precept 18: The Saints Judge the World based on two key Principles

"But when the Son of Man comes in His glory and majesty and all the angels with Him, then He will sit on the throne of His glory. All the nations will be gathered before Him [for judgment]; and He will separate them from one another, as a shepherd separates his sheep from the goats; and He will put the sheep on His right [the place of honor], and the goats on His left [the place of rejection] ...The King will answer and say to them, 'I assure you and most solemnly say to you, to the extent that you did it for one of these brothers of Mine, even the least of them, you did it for Me'" (Matthew 25:31-33, 40 AMP).

"But whoever causes one of these little ones who believe and trust in Me to stumble [that is, to sin or lose faith], it would be better for him if a heavy millstone [one requiring a donkey's strength to turn it] were hung around his neck and he were thrown into the sea" (Mark 9:42 AMP).

We were instructed to pray that his kingdom would come to the earth.

"And he said unto them, 'When ye pray, say, Our Father which art in heaven, hallowed be thy Name. Thy kingdom

come: Let thy will be done, even in earth, as it is in heaven'"
(Luke 11:2 Geneva Translation).

The kingdom has to do with ruling and law making matters. The Apostle Paul makes this clear in his first letter to the Corinthians.

> *"Do you not know that the saints (God's people) will [one day] judge the world? If the world is to be judged by you, are you not competent to try trivial (insignificant, petty) cases?" (1 Corinthians 6:2 AMP).*

> *"And the nations (Gentiles) became enraged, and Your wrath and indignation came, and the time came for the dead to be judged, and [the time came] to reward Your bondservants the prophets and the saints (God's people) and those who fear Your name, the small and the great, and [the time came] to destroy the destroyers of the earth" (Revelation 11:18 AMP).*

> *"Jesus said to them, 'I assure you and most solemnly say to you, in the renewal [that is, the Messianic restoration and regeneration of all things] when the Son of Man sits on His glorious throne, you [who have followed Me, becoming My disciples] will also sit on twelve thrones, judging the twelve tribes of Israel'" (Matthew 19:28 AMP).*

> *"that you may eat and drink at My table in My kingdom, and you will sit on thrones judging the twelve tribes of Israel" (Luke 22:30 AMP).*

This work of judgment and harvest and judgment by the Word of God can only be done through the unity of the Bride of Christ. Jesus did not tell his disciples that He would come back to convince the world. He gave that responsibility to us and said that it would require unity.

> *"I do not pray for these alone [it is not for their sake only that I make this request], but also for [all] those who [will ever] believe and trust in Me through their message, that they all may be one; just as You, Father, are in Me and I*

in You, that they also may be one in Us, so that the world may believe [without any doubt] that You sent Me" (John 17:20-21 AMP).

"As I kept looking, that horn was making war with the saints (believers) and overpowering them until the Ancient of Days came and judgment was passed in favor of the saints of the Most High [God], and the time arrived when the saints (believers) took possession of the kingdom" (Daniel 7:21-22 AMP).

How does the Ancient of Days come and reveal Himself? Through the poor, similarly as it was written in 1 Samuel:

"The Lord makes poor and makes rich; He brings low and He lifts up. "He raises up the poor from the dust, He lifts up the needy from the ash heap To make them sit with nobles, And inherit a seat of honor and glory; For the pillars of the earth are the Lord's, And He set the land on them. "He guards the feet of His godly (faithful) ones, But the wicked ones are silenced and perish in darkness; For a man shall not prevail by might" (1 Samuel 2:7-9 AMP).

Psalm 149 (AMP) Israel Invoked to Praise the Lord and execute judgment.

Praise the Lord! Sing to the Lord a new song, And praise Him in the congregation of His godly ones (believers).
Let Israel rejoice in their Maker; Let Zion's children rejoice in their King.
Let them praise His name with dancing; Let them sing praises to Him with the tambourine and lyre.
For the Lord takes pleasure in His people; He will beautify the humble with salvation. Let the godly ones exult in glory; Let them sing for joy on their beds.
Let the high praises of God be in their throats, And a two edged sword in their hands, To execute vengeance on the nations And punishment on the peoples,
To bind their kings with chains And their nobles with fetters

of iron,
To execute on them the judgment written. This is the honor
for all His godly ones.
Praise the Lord! (Hallelujah!)

Precept 19: Scriptural Advice for Harvest

God has made this promise since the beginning, from the garden, from the test of faith of Abraham and to Revelation and kept his promise for this day of trouble. The saints will be victorious. As you share, speak the truth in kindness (Proverbs 3:3).

"indeed I will greatly bless you, and I will greatly multiply your descendants like the stars of the heavens and like the sand on the seashore; and your seed shall possess the gate of their enemies [as conquerors]" (Genesis 22:17 AMP).

"Therefore I tell you, the kingdom of God will be taken away from you and given to [another] people who will produce the fruit of it. And he who falls on this Stone will be broken to pieces; but he on whom it falls will be crushed" (Matthew 21:43-44 AMP).

"And ye shall tread down the wicked; for they shall be ashes under the soles of your feet in the day that I shall do this, saith the LORD of hosts. (Malachi 4:3)."

"Let the godly ones exult in glory; Let them sing for joy on their beds. Let the high praises of God be in their throats, And a two-edged sword in their hands, To execute vengeance on the nations And punishment on the peoples, To bind their kings with chains And their nobles with fetters of iron, To execute on them the judgment written. This is the honor for all His godly ones. Praise the Lord! (Hallelujah)" (Psalm

149:5-9 AMP).

And the servant of the kingdom gave talents, good seed and a sharp sickle to his servants and told them that he would ask for an accounting of the fruits of their labor when he returned from his journey.

Pray that you are not offended and that your wineskins do not burst. Visit and fellowship with other congregations in the Spirit of unity through the bond of peace. Give extra copies of this book away and share them with others. Share the good news. For this is the mystery of the kingdom and time of renewal. It is at the door. Pray that God may enlarge your tent and set your face as flint to do his will. Go to those in prison and share this book with them. Go to the orphans, the poor and share the good news. Bind up the weak. Share this with student organizations across the world.

> *"The deliverers will ascend Mount Zion To judge the mountain of Esau, And the kingdom will be the Lord's" (Obadiah 1:21 NASB).*

Esau sold his birthright blessing to fulfill an appetite of the flesh. He had been chosen but he despised his birthright and traded it for a meal (Genesis 25). Any chosen nation that names the name of the God of their ancestors, the God of Isaac and Jacob, and rejects His blessings and despises his birthright and serves the flesh will pay the price of judgement. But if you will read the story that follows, Jacob was very wise in his dealings with his brother Esau and made peace with him (Genesis 32).

> *"Anyone who takes hold of the plow and looks back is not fit for the kingdom"*

Proverbs 15 Contrast of the righteous and the wicked

> *"A gentle answer turns away wrath, But a harsh word stirs up anger. The tongue of the wise makes knowledge pleasant, But the mouth of fools spouts foolishness. The eyes of the*

Lord are in every place, Watching the evil and the good. A soothing tongue is a tree of life, But perversion in it crushes the spirit. A fool rejects his father's discipline, But he who complies with rebuke is sensible. Great wealth is in the house of the righteous, But trouble is in the income of the wicked. The lips of the wise spread knowledge, But the hearts of fools are not so. The sacrifice of the wicked is an abomination to the Lord, But the prayer of the upright is His delight. The way of the wicked is an abomination to the Lord, But He loves the one who pursues righteousness. There is severe punishment for one who abandons the way; One who hates a rebuke will die. Sheol and Abaddon lie open before the Lord, How much more the hearts of mankind! A scoffer does not love one who rebukes him; He will not go to the wise. A joyful heart makes a cheerful face, But when the heart is sad, the spirit is broken. The mind of the intelligent seeks knowledge, But the mouth of fools feeds on foolishness. All the days of the needy are bad, But a cheerful heart has a continual feast. Better is a little with the fear of the Lord Than great treasure, and turmoil with the treasure. Better is a portion of vegetables where there is love, Than a fattened ox served with hatred. A hottempered person stirs up strife, But the slow to anger calms a dispute. The way of the lazy one is like a hedge of thorns, But the path of the upright is a highway. A wise son makes a father glad, But a foolish man despises his mother. Foolishness is joy to one who lacks sense, But a person of understanding walks straight. Without consultation, plans are frustrated, But with many counselors they succeed. A person has joy in an apt answer, And how delightful is a timely word! The path of life leads upward for the wise, So that he may keep away from Sheol below. The Lord will tear down the house of the proud, But He will set the boundary of the widow. Evil plans are an abomination to the Lord, But pleasant words are pure. He who profits illicitly troubles his own house, But he who hates bribes will live. The heart of the righteous ponders how to answer, But the mouth of the wicked pours out evil things. The Lord is far from the wicked, But He hears the prayer of the righteous. Bright eyes gladden the heart; Good news refreshes the bones. One whose ear listens to a lifegiving rebuke Will stay amon g the wise. One who neglects discipline rejects himself, But on e who listens to a rebuke acquires understanding. The fear o f the Lord is the instruction for wisdom, And before hono r comes humility" (Proverbs 15 NASB).

89

"Like apples of gold in settings of silver Is a word spoken at the right time. Like an earring of gold and an ornament of fine gold Is a wise reprove to an ear that listens and learns. Like the cold of snow [brought from the mountains] in the time of harvest, So is a faithful messenger to those who send him; For he refreshes the life of his masters" (Proverbs 25:1-13 AMP).

Considering the harvest and judgement

"I say to you, whoever declares openly and confesses Me before men [speaking freely of Me as his Lord], the Son of Man also will declare openly and confess him [as one of His own] before the angels of God. But he who denies Me before men will be denied in the presence of the angels of God" (Luke 12:89 AMP).

Any man or woman that does not judge righteously nor is merciful to the poor and little one, does not have a place of authority in the kingdom of heaven on the earth. They will be cast out of their place of authority and gnash their teeth in jealousy. Their robes must be white with the work and fruit of righteousness and of the Spirit to be qualified for service. They must worship the Lamb of God who sits upon the throne in heaven at the right hand of God the Father and give Him respect ("kiss the Son"—Psalm 2). They must serve Him in righteousness and truth (See the Judgment in Matthew 25:30-40).

You are the angels of the kingdom of heaven. Your citizenship is in heaven.

Your authority is there and here. What you bind in heaven is bound in the earth, so long as it is in agreement with the Word of God. This is our Lord's harvest. The Father delights in giving the kingdom to His children.

"Those who sow in tears shall harvest with joyful shouting" (Psalm 126:5 NASB).

Do not watch the clouds

"One who watches the wind will not sow and one who looks at the clouds will not harvest" (Ecclesiastes 11:4 NASB).

If you are looking to the wind and clouds and waiting on Jesus to show up and rescue you, you will be waiting a long time. He set you in this place at this time to do His work. The gifts and callings of God are irrevocable. He comes in the clouds to harvest the earth. We are that cloud of witnesses together with the testimony of the saints past. We arise to shake the earth with the thunder of His voice in unity and thrust in the sharp sickle of His fiery Word for harvest. We are His bride. He asks us to deliver the nations to Him and put them under His feet.

"then comes the end, when He hands over the kingdom to our God and Father, when He has abolished all rule and all authority and power. For He must reign until He has put all His enemies under His feet. The last enemy that will be abolished is death" (1 Corinthians 15:2426 NASB).

"You will multiply the nation, You will increase their joy; They will rejoice in Your presence As with the joy of harvest, As people rejoice when they divide the spoils" (Isaiah 9:3 NASB).

"The Lord has sworn by His right hand and by His mighty arm: "I will never again give your grain as food for your enemies, Nor will foreigners drink your new wine for which you have labored." But those who harvest it will eat it and praise the Lord; And those who gather it will drink it in the courtyards of My sanctuary. Go through, go through the gates, Clear a way for the people! Build up, build up the highway, Remove the stones, lift up a flag over the peoples" (Isaiah 62:810 NASB).

"Put in the sickle, for the harvest is ripe. Come, tread the grapes, for the wine press is full; The vats overflow, for their wickedness is great" (Joel 3:13 NASB).

"Allow both to grow together until the harvest; and at the time of the harvest I will say to the reapers, 'First gather up the weeds and bind them in bundles to burn them; but

gather the wheat into my barn (Matthew 13:30 NASB).'"

Remember that the fire that burns in judgment to test the works of men is the Word of God.

> *"and the field is the world; and as for the good seed, these are the sons of the kingdom; and the weeds are the sons of the evil one; and the enemy who sowed them is the devil, and the harvest is the end of the age; and the reapers are angels. So just as the weeds are **gathered up and burned with fire**, so shall it be at the end of the age (Matthew 13:38-40 NASB)."*

It has been said that the Bible is a self-referential text

We have wrongly assumed that the word angel always refers literally to the angelic creatures that descend upon the earth from heaven as God's messengers. We must consider that there are four Rabbinic ways to interpret scripture. I will leave you to explore this on your own if you wish. To conclude that Jesus was referring to the angelic in the parable of the sower would discount the fact that He spoke of sending "laborers" into the field, that is the world (Matthew 13:38 AMP). It would also disregard the many scriptures shared in this book that refer to the saints performing the work of harvest and judgment. This riddle has protected the saints until the proper time.

> *"And I heard a voice from heaven, saying, "Write: 'Blessed are the dead who die in the Lord from now on!'" "Yes," says the Spirit, "so that they may rest from their labors, for their deeds follow with them." Then I looked, and behold, a white cloud, and sitting on the cloud was one like a son of man, with a golden crown on His head and a sharp sickle in His hand. And another angel came out of the temple, calling out with a loud voice to Him who sat on the cloud, "Put in your sickle and reap, for the hour to reap has come, because the harvest of the earth is ripe" (Revelation 14:13-15 NASB).*

He is supported by a cloud of saints. The saints and the elect are revealed to the earth from heaven in a flame of fire [of the judgement of the Word of God] upon the earth.

"and to give relief to you who are so distressed and to us as well when the Lord Jesus is revealed from heaven with His mighty angels in a flame of fire," (2 Thessalonians 1:7 AMP).

Go now into the fields

"I have leaned on you since my birth; You are He who took me from my mother's womb; My praise is continually of You. I have become a marvel to many, For You are my strong refuge. My mouth is filled with Your praise And with Your glory all day long" (Psalm 71:68 NASB).

"My tongue also will tell of Your righteousness all day long; For they are put to shame, for they are humiliated who seek my harm" (Psalm 71:24 NASB).

"For the sorrow that is according to the will of God produces a repentance without regret, leading to salvation, but the sorrow of the world produces death" (2 Corinthians 7:10 NASB)

"Nations will see and be ashamed, deprived of all their power. They will put their hands over their mouths and their ears will become deaf" (Micah 7:16 NIV).

"And many peoples and powerful nations will come to Jerusalem to seek the Lord Almighty and to entreat him" (Zechariah 8:22 NIV).

"Their descendants will be known among the nations and their offspring among the peoples. All who see them will acknowledge that they are a people the Lord has blessed" (Isaiah 61:9 NIV).

Precept 20: The Gifts and Callings of God Are Irrevocable

"See then the kindness and severity of God: to those who fell, severity, but to you, God's kindness, if you continue in His kindness; for otherwise you too will be cut off. And they also, if they do not continue in their unbelief, will be grafted in; for God is able to graft them in again. For if you were cut off from what is by nature a wild olive tree, and contrary to nature were grafted into a cultivated olive tree, how much more will these who are the natural branches be grafted into their own olive tree? For I do not want you, brothers and sisters, to be uninformed of this mystery—so that you will not be wise in your own estimation—that a partial hardening has happened to Israel until the fullness of the Gentiles has come in; and so all Israel will be saved; just as it is written:

'The Deliverer will come from Zion, He will remove ungodliness from Jacob.' "This is My covenant with them, When I take away their sins.'

"In relation to the gospel they are enemies on your account, but in relation to God's choice they are beloved on account of the fathers; **for the gifts and the calling of God are irrevocable.** *For just as you once were disobedient to God, but now have been shown mercy because of their disobedience, so these also now have been disobedient, that because of the mercy shown to you they also may now be shown mercy. For God has shut up all in disobedience, so that He*

*may show mercy to all. Oh, the depth of the riches, both of
the wisdom and knowledge of God! How unsearchable are
His judgments and unfathomable His ways! For who has
known the mind of the Lord, or who became His counselor?
Or who has first given to Him, that it would be paid back
to him? For from Him, and through Him, and to Him are
all things. To Him be the glory forever. Amen" (Romans
11:22-36 NASB).*

*"I advise you to buy from Me gold refined by fire so that
you may become rich, and white garments so that you may
clothe yourself and the shame of your nakedness will not be
revealed; and eye salve to apply to your eyes so that you may
see. Those whom I love, I rebuke and discipline; therefore be
zealous and repent. Behold, I stand at the door and knock; if
anyone hears My voice and opens the door, I will come in to
him and will dine with him, and he with Me. The one who
overcomes, I will grant to him to sit with Me on My throne,
as I also overcame and sat with My Father on His throne.
The one who has an ear, let him hear what the Spirit says to
the churches'" (Revelation 3:18-22 NASB).*

I am reminded again of the words of the Apostle Paul to the Ephesians that we are "seated with Christ in the heavenlies" and in another
place, "we are citizens of heaven." Then I recalled the words of Jesus in
Matthew.

*"Jesus said to them, 'I assure you and most solemnly say to
you, in the renewal [that is, the Messianic restoration and
regeneration of all things] when the Son of Man sits on His
glorious throne, you [who have followed Me, becoming My
disciples] will also sit on twelve thrones, judging the twelve
tribes of Israel'" (Matthew 19:28 AMP).*

*"But the Helper (Comforter, Advocate, Intercessor —Coun-
selor, Strengthener, Standby), the Holy Spirit, whom the
Father will send in My name [in My place, to represent Me
and act on My behalf], He will teach you all things. And
He will help you remember everything that I have told you"
(John 14:26 AMP).*

"Call to Me and I will answer you, and tell you [and even

show you] great and mighty things, [things which have been confined and hidden], which you do not know and understand and cannot distinguish." (Jeremiah 33:3 AMP).

"Blessed be the Lord, my Rock and my great strength, Who trains my hands for war And my fingers for battle; My [steadfast] lovingkindness and my fortress, My high tower and my rescuer, My shield and He in whom I take refuge, Who subdues my people under me. Lord, what is man that You take notice of him? Or the son of man that You think of him?" (Psalm 144:13).

And again to the words of the Jesus, the Messiah:

"Now I say to you, everyone who confesses Me before people, the Son of Man will also confess him before the angels of God; but the one who denies Me before people will be denied before the angels of God. And everyone who speaks a word against the Son of Man, it will be forgiven him; but the one who blasphemes against the Holy Spirit, it will not be forgiven him. Now when they bring you before the synagogues and the officials and the authorities, do not worry about how or what you are to speak in your defense, or what you are to say; for the Holy Spirit will teach you in that very hour what you ought to say" (Luke 12:8-12 NASB).

Consider the above verse carefully and prayerfully with the following verse as you try to break it down. Perhaps we have made some assumptions about the way Jesus spoke about Himself and the disciples. For example, when He said that they would "see" Him again, He was referring to the Gift of the Holy Spirit." If we compare the above verse with the one below, it appears that Jesus is referring to two different people. One who is a Christian leader, led by the Holy Spirit at the end of the tribulation and the Holy Spirit which testifies of Jesus and will not forgive those who don't believe in Christ having come from God.

"Beloved, do not believe every spirit, but test the spirits to see whether they are from God, because many false prophets have gone out into the world. By this you know the Spirit of

God: every spirit that confesses that Jesus Christ has come in the flesh is from God; and every spirit that does not confess Jesus is not from God; this is the spirit of the antichrist, which you have heard is coming, and now it is already in the world. You are from God, little children, and have overcome them; because greater is He who is in you than he who is in the world. They are from the world, therefore they speak as from the world, and the world listens to them. We are from God. The one who knows God listens to us; the one who is not from God does not listen to us. By this we know the spirit of truth and the spirit of error. Beloved, let's love one another; for love is from God, and everyone who loves has been born of God and knows God. The one who does not love does not know God, because God is love. By this the love of God was revealed in us, that God has sent His only Son into the world so that we may live through Him. In this is love, not that we loved God, but that He loved us and sent His Son to be the propitiation for our sins. Beloved, if God so loved us, we also ought to love one another. No one has ever seen God; if we love one another, God remains in us, and His love is perfected in us. By this we know that we remain in Him and He in us, because He has given to us of His Spirit. We have seen and testify that the Father has sent the Son to be the Savior of the world. Whoever confesses that Jesus is the Son of God, God remains in him, and he in God. We have come to know and have believed the love which God has for us. God is love, and the one who remains in love remains in God, and God remains in him. By this, love is perfected with us, so that we may have confidence in the day of judgment; because as He is, we also are in this world. There is no fear in love, but perfect love drives out fear, because fear involves punishment, and the one who fears is not perfected in love. We love, because He first loved us. If someone says, "I love God," and yet he hates his brother or sister, he is a liar; for the one who does not love his brother and sister whom he has seen, cannot love God, whom he has not seen. And this commandment we have from Him, that the one who loves God must also love his brother and sister" (1 John 4 NASB).

Precept 21: Is Jesus Christ coming back soon? Revisiting scripture

There are several scriptures that must be considered together when asking this question. Additionally, they must all agree together. If they do not, then we must go with the majority rule or perhaps even consider a riddle that is unclear. We must focus on what is clear.

Don't look to the clouds during sowing and harvest

> "He who watches the wind [waiting for all conditions to be perfect] will not sow [seed], and he who looks at the clouds will not reap [a harvest]" (Ecclesiastes 11:4 AMP).

Christians looking to the sky will not participate in harvest. Waiting for all conditions to be perfect is not the mark of a bold Christian. We must be bold in this hour.

The testimony of the two angels

> "And after He said these things, He was caught up as they looked on, and a cloud took Him up out of their sight. While they were looking intently into the sky as He was going, two men in white clothing suddenly stood beside them, who said, 'Men of Galilee, why do you stand looking into the sky? This

[same] Jesus, who has been taken up from you into heaven, will return in just the same way as you have watched Him go into heaven"' (Acts 1:911 AMP).

Waiting for Jesus to return and fix things is like the man in the parable of the talents that buried his talent in the ground. Jesus is away. We will be asked for an accounting of our work. We must consider also that God puts no confidence in the counsel of His angels:

"God puts no trust or confidence even in His [Heavenly] servants, And He charges His angels with error" (Job 4:18 AMP).

"For after all it is only just for God to repay with distress those who distress you, and to give relief to you who are so distressed and to us as well when the Lord Jesus is revealed from heaven with His mighty angels in a flame of fire, dealing out [full and complete] vengeance to those who do not [seek to] know God and to those who ignore and refuse to obey the gospel of our Lord Jesus [by choosing not to respond to Him]" (2 Thessalonians 1:68 AMP).

The angel in Acts chapter one said that Jesus would return in the same way he left. He did not say when. In Matthew 13 below Jesus says the harvest is the end of the age and that the reapers are the angels (the saints—the laborers). In the above verse Paul says that Jesus will be revealed from heaven with his angels in flames of fire. As we discussed previously, all truth is revealed from above, from God in heaven. Jesus will be revealed from above to all as having been sent by God through his mighty angels, the saints, to fulfill His prayer in John 17:

"I in them and You in Me, that they may be perfected and completed into one, so that the world may know [without any doubt] that You sent Me, and [that You] have loved them, just as You have loved Me" (John 17:23 AMP).

I have to believe Jesus over the angels in Acts chapter one regarding what happens during the time of harvest. Jesus may very well come at some point just as the angels said. I do know that the saints must bind the wicked and bring the wheat into the barn. It is up to the Body of Christ, the Christian believers—in unity—to convince the world. Additionally, Jesus said in John 17, "I go to the Father." He left the disciples in charge of His message.

Jesus does not perform the harvest, the saints do. That means you and I. We must be salt and light in the courthouse, on the street corner, in the prison, in the orphanage, to the sick and the lame and to the poor and especially the heads of the nations.

It was also prophesied by Moses and retold by Jude

> *"And he said, 'The LORD came from Sinai, And rose up from Seir unto them; he shined forth from mount Paran, and he came with ten thousand of saints; from his right hand went a fiery law for them'" (Deuteronomy 33:2 AKJV).*

Moses was the first to prophecy the end and the inheritance of the saints. Thousands would work in unity and God would send before them a fiery law, the Word that would test the works of men, righteous and unrighteous alike.

> *"Then He said to His disciples, 'The harvest is [indeed] plentiful, but the workers are few. So pray to the Lord of the harvest to send out workers into His harvest'" (Matthew 9:37-38 AMP).*

When is the harvest? It is the end of the age

> *"and the field is the world; and [as for] the good seed, these are the sons of the kingdom; and the weeds are the sons of the evil one; and the enemy who sowed them is the devil, and the harvest is the end of the age; and the reapers are angels. So just as the weeds are gathered up and burned in the fire, so will it be at the end of the age" (Matthew 13:38-40 AMP).*

Remember that even the angels did not completely understand everything

It was revealed to them that their services [their prophecies regarding grace] were not [meant] for themselves and their time, but for you, in these things [the death, resurrection, and glorification of Jesus Christ] which have now been told to you by those who preached the gospel to you by the [power of the] Holy Spirit [who was] sent from heaven. Into these things even the angels long to look" (1 Peter 1:12 AMP).

Do not be complacent

> *"Do this, knowing that this is a critical time. It is already the hour for you to awaken from your sleep [of spiritual complacency]; for our salvation is nearer to us now than when we first believed [in Christ]. The night [this present evil age] is almost gone and the day [of Christ's return] is almost here. So let us fling away the works of darkness and put on the [full] armor of light. Let us conduct ourselves properly and honorably as in the [light of] day, not in carousing and drunkenness, not in sexual promiscuity and irresponsibility, not in quarreling and jealousy" (Romans 13:11-13 AMP).*

Complacency and idleness is sin

> *"Your eyes are too pure to approve evil, And You cannot look favorably on wickedness. Why then do You look favorably On those who act treacherously? Why are you silent when the wicked (Chaldean oppressors) destroy Those more righteous than they?" (Habakkuk 1:13 AMP).*

> *"Through laziness the rafters [of state affairs] decay and the roof sags, and through idleness [the roof of] the house leaks" (Ecclesiastes 10:18 AMP).*

State affairs are the business of the Church. The Body of Christ must be involved in the judicial system and politics. The Word of God makes this clear.

Jesus is revealed from heaven to the earth through His servants, the saints

"For after all it is only just for God to repay with distress those who distress you, and to give relief to you who are so distressed and to us as well when the Lord Jesus is revealed from heaven with His mighty angels in a flame of fire, dealing out [full and complete] vengeance to those who do not [seek to] know God and to those who ignore and refuse to obey the gospel of our Lord Jesus [by choosing not to respond to Him]" (2 Thessalonians 1:6-8 AMP).

We must remember that we are reading "riddles" many times in scripture. The "angels" are His servants, the "laborers in the field" in another scripture; and "in a flame of fire" refers to the judgment written in the Word of God concerning those who ignore and refuse to obey. It is up to the Body of Christ to bring distress upon the wicked and remove them from power.

"I kept looking Until thrones were set up, And the Ancient of Days (God) took His seat His garment was white as snow And the hair of His head like pure wool. His throne was flames of fire; Its wheels were a burning fire" (Daniel 7:9 AMP).

"Do you not know that the saints (God's people) will [one day] judge the world? If the world is to be judged by you, are you not competent to try trivial (insignificant, petty) cases?" (1 Corinthians 6:2 AMP).

Jesus does come in the clouds (Hebrews 12:1) of His body the church, thousands of His saints (Jude 1), a great cloud of witnesses and their testimonies past and present—through his ministering flames of fire—which are the saints along with the testimony and faith of those who have gone before. Their faith rises from the dust and speaks.

"By faith Abel brought God a better offering than Cain did. By faith he was commended as righteous, when God spoke

well of his offerings. And by faith Abel still speaks, even though he is dead" (Hebrews 11:4 AMP).

Jesus does bring everything under His feet through His body the Church

"After that comes the end (completion), when He hands over the kingdom to God the Father, after He has made inoperative and abolished every ruler and every authority and power. For Christ must reign [as King] until He has put all His enemies under His feet" (1 Corinthians 15:24-25 AMP).

This is the word that the chosen king in the earth must keep and the body of Christ must keep "until the end" spoken of in Revelation. Every ruler and authority must be brought under Christ's feet.

"And he who overcomes [the world through believing that Jesus is the Son of God] and he who keeps My deeds [doing things that please Me] until the [very] end, to him I will give authority and power over the nations; and he shall shepherd and rule them with a rod of iron, as the earthen pots are broken in pieces, as I also have received authority [and power to rule them] from My Father" (Revelation 2:26-27 AMP).

Every eye shall see Him, that is, perceive and see the truth of who He is and the work He has done on the cross when they are persuaded by the clouds of saints in the earth that unite and fulfill Jesus' high priestly prayer.

"Behold, He is coming with the clouds, and every eye will see Him, even those who pierced Him; and all the tribes (nations) of the earth will mourn over Him [realizing their sin and guilt, and anticipating the coming wrath]. So it is to be. Amen" (Revelation 1:7 AMP)

"But when the Son of Man comes in His glory and majesty and all the angels with Him, then He will sit on the throne of His glory. All the nations will be gathered before Him [for judgment]; and He will separate them from one another, as a shepherd separates his sheep from the goats; and He will put the sheep on His right [the place of honor], and the goats on His left [the place of rejection]. Then the King will say to those on His right, 'Come, you blessed of My Father [you favored of God, appointed to eternal salvation], inherit the kingdom prepared for you from the foundation of the world. For I was hungry, and you gave Me something to eat; I was thirsty, and you gave Me something to drink; I was a stranger, and you invited Me in; I was naked, and you clothed Me; I was sick, and you visited Me [with help and ministering care]; I was in prison, and you came to Me [ignoring personal danger].' Then the righteous will answer Him, 'Lord, when did we see You hungry, and feed You, or thirsty, and give You something to drink? And when did we see You as a stranger, and invite You in, or naked, and clothe You? And when did we see You sick, or in prison, and come to You?' The King will answer and say to them, 'I assure you and most solemnly say to you, to the extent that you did it for one of these brothers of Mine, even the least of them, you did it for Me.' "Then He will say to those on His left, 'Leave Me, you cursed ones, into the eternal fire which has been prepared for the devil and his angels (demons); for I was hungry, and you gave Me nothing to eat; I was thirsty, and you gave Me nothing to drink; I was a stranger, and you did not invite Me in; naked, and you did not clothe Me; sick, and in prison, and you did not visit Me [with help and ministering care].' Then they also [in their turn] will answer, 'Lord, when did we see You hungry, or thirsty, or as a stranger, or naked, or sick, or in prison, and did not minister to You?' Then He will reply to them, 'I assure you and most solemnly say to you, to the extent that you did not do it for one of the least of these [my followers], you did not do it for Me.' Then these [unbelieving people] will go away into eternal (unending) punishment, but those who are righteous and in right standing with God [will go, by His remarkable grace] into eternal (unending) life" (Matthew 25:31-46 AMP).

The peacemakers will be lifted up on the shoulders of the people and celebrated (this is the picture of the Jewish wedding feast when the bride and groom are seated on chairs and lifted up and carried around the room while the guests sing and celebrate). The celebration in question will be the union of heaven and earth. "Thy kingdom come, thy will be done, on earth as it is in heaven."

♪ Pause and listen to *End of the Age: Book Four, "Blessed are the Peacemakers."*
♪

> *"And He raised us up together with Him [when we believed], and seated us with Him in the heavenly places, [because we are] in Christ Jesus" (Ephesians 2:6 AMP).*

He gathers his elect from the four winds with the sound of a clear trumpet blast calling the saints to battle—to prepare for the harvest of the end. He provides them with a sharp sickle for harvest. The reason we read "appear in the sky" is because the truth of God's word and chosen servants is revealed "from heaven," as we discussed before.

> *"And at that time the sign of the Son of Man [coming in His glory] will appear in the sky, and then all the tribes of the earth [and especially Israel] will mourn [regretting their rebellion and rejection of the Messiah], and they will see the Son of Man coming on the clouds of heaven with power and great glory [in brilliance and splendor]. And He will send His angels with a loud trumpet and they will gather together His elect (God's chosen ones) from the four winds, from one end of the heavens to the other" (Matthew 24:30-31 AMP).*

Jesus is spiritually revealed in the Word of God through His Body the Church and in the opening of the books which he does for the saints at the end of the age. The books are opened to our understanding. Israel morns in sackcloth—a symbol of repentance ("the sun turns black") and the Son of Man gathers the angels (the elect) for harvest.

The reaping of the earth

Paul explained that we are Christ's body (1 Corinthians 12:27). The world must be brought under His heavenly footstool where He sits today at the right hand of God the Father in heaven. This happens at the reaping. As for the riddle of the "white cloud" below, it makes sense that it would refer to a cloud of saints.

> *"Again I looked, and this is what I saw: a white cloud, and sitting on the cloud was One like the Son of Man, with a crown of gold on His head and a sharp sickle [of swift judgment] in His hand. And another angel came out of the temple, calling with a loud voice to Him who was sitting upon the cloud, 'Put in Your sickle and reap [at once], for the hour to reap [in judgment] has arrived, because the earth's harvest is fully ripened.' So He who was sitting on the cloud cast His sickle over the earth, and the earth was reaped (judged)" (Revelation 14:14-16 AMP).*

A man, a believer in Christ with God-given Davidic authority (hence the crown of gold), seated with and supported by a cloud of saints, thrusts his sickle into the earth to judge the wicked.

> *"Put in the sickle [of judgment], for the harvest is ripe; Come, tread [the grapes], for the wine press is full; The vats overflow, for the wickedness [of the people] is great. Multitudes, multitudes in the valley of decision (judgment)! For the day of the Lord is near in the valley of decision [when judgment is executed]. The sun and the moon grow dark And the stars lose their brightness. The Lord thunders and roars from Zion And utters His voice from Jerusalem [in judgment of His enemies], And the heavens and the earth tremble and shudder; But the Lord is a refuge for His people And a stronghold [of protection] to the children of Israel. Then you will know and understand fully that I am the Lord your God, Dwelling in Zion, My holy mountain. Then Jerusalem will be holy, And strangers [who do not belong] will no longer pass through it" (Joel 3:13-17 AMP).*

Precept 22: The King above rules from heaven

According to some, and as indicated by some of the scriptures shared below, Jesus will not return until Israel confesses Jesus as its Lord and Savior. That will depend on us acting in unity and not so fragmented as we are now. Unity, as I said before, was Jesus' prayer for us in John 17. Inheriting the Kingdom as Jesus says to us is dependent on just that: unity. From the promise to Abraham, the Song of Moses (the fiery law that goes before the holy ones), to Daniel where the saints possess the kingdoms, to the promises of Jesus and the thrones established for the millennial reign in Revelation: it all depends on the unity of believing Gentiles.

Come and inherit the kingdom prepared for you from the foundation of the world" (Matthew 25:34 AMP).

King Jesus went to the Father and remains in heaven; His work is complete.

*"But now I am coming to You; and I say these things [while I am still] in the world so that they may experience **My joy made full and complete** and perfect within them [filling their hearts with My delight]" (John 17:13 AMP).*

"After that comes the end (completion), when He hands over the kingdom to God the Father, after He has made

inoperative and abolished every ruler and every authority and power. For Christ must reign [as King] until He has put all His enemies under His feet. The last enemy to be abolished and put to an end is death" (1 Corinthians 15:24-26 AMP).

Do we have a part in ending the authority of every ruler? Absolutely. We are the clouds that come with Him. For He is already here (F.B. Meyer). We are to rise up in His strength and speak His words as you will see if you have not already.

"The Son is the radiance and only expression of the glory of [our awesome] God [reflecting God's Shekinah glory, the Lightbeing, the brilliant light of the divine], and the exact representation and perfect imprint of His [Father's] essence, and upholding and maintaining and propelling all things [the entire physical and spiritual universe] by His powerful word [carrying the universe along to its predetermined goal]. When He [Himself and no other] had [by offering Himself on the cross as a sacrifice for sin] accomplished purification from sins and established our freedom from guilt, He sat down [revealing His completed work] at the right hand of the Majesty on high [revealing His Divine authority]" (Hebrews 1:3 AMP).

The ones beneath overcome the world and believe that Jesus is the Son of God.

"And he who overcomes [the world through believing that Jesus is the Son of God] and he who keeps My deeds [doing things that please Me] until the [very] end, to him I will give authority and power over the nations" (Revelation 2:26 AMP).

"Ask of Me, and I will assuredly give [You] the nations as Your inheritance, And the ends of the earth as Your possession" (Psalm 2:8 AMP).

"He who overcomes [the world through believing that Jesus

110

is the Son of God], I will grant to him [the privilege] to sit beside Me on My throne, as I also overcame and sat down beside My Father on His throne" (Revelation 3:21 AMP).

"Then the King will say to those on His right, 'Come, you blessed of My Father [you favored of God, appointed to eternal salvation], inherit the kingdom prepared for you from the foundation of the world'"(Matthew 25:34 AMP).

We are His angels, servants and warriors called to do His Kingdom work

"Alas! for that day is great, There is none like it; It is the time of Jacob's [unequaled] trouble, But he will be saved from it. 'It shall come about on that day,' says the Lord of hosts, 'that I will break the yoke off your neck and I will tear off your bonds and force apart your shackles; and strangers will no longer make slaves of the people [of Israel]. 'But they shall serve the Lord their God and [the descendant of] David their King, whom I will raise up for them'" (Jeremiah 30:7-9 AMP).

"My [steadfast] lovingkindness and my fortress, My high tower and my rescuer, My shield and He in whom I take refuge, Who subdues my people under me" (Psalm 144:2 AMP).

"Then I said, 'Behold, I come [to the throne] ; In the scroll of the book it is written of me'" (Psalm 40:7 AMP).

"but when it is time for the trumpet call of the seventh angel, when he is about to sound, then the mystery of God [that is, His hidden purpose and plan] is finished, as He announced the gospel to His servants the prophets" (Revelation 10:7 AMP).

We must remember that Israel was called to be a nation of king priests at Mt. Sinai. The apostle Peter tells us that we are a Royal (kingly) priesthood. That involves two roles: 1) executing justice and judgment in the city gates of the earth, and 2) serving as priests to lead people to peace with God through Jesus Christ and disciple them. We must also remember that the kingdom would be taken from Israel and given to a nation with the works of repentance.

Why is this so? To provoke Israel to jealously and convince them that Jesus is their Savior, the one they have rejected.

"But now I am speaking to you who are Gentiles. In as much then as I am an apostle to the Gentiles, I magnify my ministry, in the hope of somehow making my fellow countrymen jealous [by stirring them up so that they will seek the truth] and perhaps save some of them. For if their [present] rejection [of salvation] is for the reconciliation of the world [to God], what will their acceptance [of salvation] be but [nothing less than] life from the dead? If the first portion [of dough offered as the first fruits] is holy, so is the whole batch; and if the root (Abraham, the patriarchs) is holy, so are the branches (the Israelites). But if some of the branches were broken off, and you [Gentiles], being like a wild olive shoot, were grafted in among them to share with them the rich root of the olive tree, do not boast over the [broken] branches and exalt yourself at their expense. If you do boast and feel superior, remember that it is not you who supports the root, but the root that supports you. You will say then, "Branches were broken off so that I might be grafted in." That is true. They were broken off because of their unbelief, but you stand by your faith [as believers understanding the truth of Christ's deity]. Do not be conceited, but [rather stand in great awe of God and] fear [Him]; for if God did not spare the natural branches [because of unbelief], He will not spare you either" (Romans 11:13-21 AMP).

It was ordained by God that the Jews would reject Jesus so that his message of salvation would go to the Gentiles. According to Messianic Jewish Teacher Kevin Geoffrey quoting the Apostle Paul, the Gentiles (those non-Jewish), must be saved and unified in such a way as to provoke them to jealously. Only then will the "end" come.

"For that is what the Lord has commanded us, saying, 'I have placed You as a light for the Gentiles, So that You may bring [the message of eternal] salvation to the end of the earth'" (Acts 13:47 AMP).

"'O Jerusalem, Jerusalem, who murders the prophets and stones [to death] those [messengers] who are sent to her [by God]! How often I wanted to gather your children together [around Me], as a hen gathers her chicks under her wings, and you were unwilling. Listen carefully: your house is being left to you desolate [completely abandoned by God and destitute of His protection]! For I say to you, you will not see Me again [ministering to you publicly] until you say, 'Blessed [to be celebrated with praise] is He who comes in the name of the Lord!'" (Matthew 23:37-39 AMP).

So, don't wait for Jesus. Don't wait for tribulation. Share your testimony. Be unified, not fragmented. Share your testimony and how Jesus has changed your life in every way possible.

Precept 23: The Mountains of Type and Shadow, of Reality and Truth

Mt. Moriah

In Genesis 22, Abraham was called from paganism and tested by offering his son of promise to God as a burnt offering. He believed that God would provide. God did provide a ram in the thicket, a type and shadow of the sacrifice of Jesus Christ on the cross. Because of Abraham's faith, God made him a promise. His faith and obedience was counted to him as righteousness.

Mt. Sinai

In Exodus 19-20, Moses speaks to God face to face on the mountain in fire and smoke. The old covenant of the Ten Commandments is established—five dealing with our relationship with God and five dealing with our relationship with men. Jesus referenced this dichotomy of the Ten Commandments when He condensed the commandments into what He called the great commandments: 1) Love the Lord your God with all your heart, mind and strength and 2) love your neighbor as yourself. The Ten Commandments was a tutor to bring us to the new covenant in Jesus Christ, a covenant of the new creation where the law of God is written on our hearts by the Holy Spirit—where God takes from us our heart of stone and rebellion and gives us a new heart off flesh and quickens our spirit to make us alive unto eternal life. For God does not desire to dwell in a tent or in buildings made by men. His desire is to dwell within the hearts of men.

The Hill of Golgotha

God the Father sent His son, born by the seed of the Word of God from the womb of the Virgin Mary. He lived a sinless earthly life, though tempted in every way as we are. He was crucified at the age of 33, died and was buried. On the third day he rose again from the dead. His body did not see corruption. After being seen by many witnesses and commissioning them, he ascended into heaven where He sat down at the right hand of the Father, having completed His work in the earth. He sent the Holy Spirit, the Parecletos, the Comforter, to remind us of what He had taught us and to show us the things to come.

Mt. Zion and the Davidic Covenant

Mt. Zion is many things, all resting on the foundation of Christ. Christ is the solid rock, the true Shepherd, the corner stone, the firm foundation, the Lamb within the holy city of living stones, God dwelling within His people by the New Covenant in His Blood, the Light of the World, the Light of the Holy City and the New Jerusalem. Resting on this foundation are the twelve foundations of the apostles. Resting on the twelve foundations of the apostles are the cloud of witnesses past and present, the house and city of living stones, the true spiritual descendants of Abraham in the faith, a nation of kings and priests, the heavenly Jerusalem, the peacemakers, the inheritors of judgment who shall possess the city gates of the land, the reapers, the city on the hill, the mountain of God's house. And finally, the capstone, Jesus Christ. To Him be all honor and glory forever and ever.

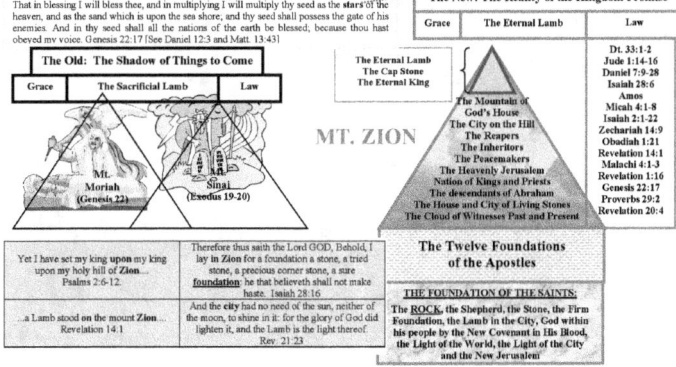

But you have come to <u>Mount Zion</u>, **to the heavenly Jerusalem, the city of the living God.** You have come to thousands upon thousands of angels in joyful assembly, to the church of the firstborn, whose names are written in heaven. You have come to God, the judge of all men, to the spirits of righteous men made perfect, to Jesus the mediator of a new covenant, and to the sprinkled blood that speaks of a better word than the blood of Abel. See to it that you do not refuse him who speaks. If they did not escape when they refused him who warned them on earth, how much less will we, if we turn away from him who warns us from heaven? At that time his voice shook the earth, but now he has promised, "Once more I will shake not only the earth but also the heavens." The words "once more" indicate the removing of what can be shaken—that is, created things—so that which cannot be shaken may remain. Therefore, since **we are receiving a kingdom** that cannot be shaken, let us be thankful, and so worship God acceptably with reverence and awe, for our "God is a consuming fire." Hebrews 12:22-29 NIV

The Inheritance of the Kingdom
(Hebrews 12:22-29; Romans 4:13; Revelation 20:4; Psalms 9:16; Psalms 141:10; Revelation 17:17)

... the Ancient of days came, and judgment was given to the saints of the most High; and the time came that the saints possessed the kingdom. Daniel 7:22
And they that be wise shall shine as the brightness of the firmament; and they that turn many to righteousness as the **stars** for ever and ever. Daniel 12:3

That in blessing I will bless thee, and in multiplying I will multiply thy seed as the stars of the heaven, and as the sand which is upon the sea shore; and thy seed shall possess the gate of his enemies. And in thy seed shall all the nations of the earth be blessed; because thou hast obeyed my voice. Genesis 22:17 [See Daniel 12:3 and Matt. 13:43]

The New: The Reality of the Kingdom Promise

Grace	The Eternal Lamb	Law

The Old: The Shadow of Things to Come

Grace	The Sacrificial Lamb	Law

Mt. Moriah (Genesis 22)

Sinai (Exodus 19-20)

The Eternal Lamb
The Cap Stone
The Eternal King

MT. ZION

The Mountain of God's House
The City on the Hill
The Reapers
The Inheritors
The Peacemakers
The Heavenly Jerusalem
Nation of Kings and Priests
The descendants of Abraham
The House and City of Living Stones
The Cloud of Witnesses Past and Present

Dt. 33:1-2
Jude 1:14-16
Daniel 7:9-28
Isaiah 28:6
Amos
Micah 4:1-8
Isaiah 2:1-22
Zechariah 14:9
Obadiah 1:21
Revelation 14:1
Malachi 4:1-3
Revelation 1:16
Genesis 22:17
Proverbs 29:2
Revelation 20:4

Yet I have set my king **upon** my king upon my holy hill of **Zion**...
Psalms 2:6-12.

...a Lamb stood on the mount **Zion**...
Revelation 14:1

Therefore thus saith the Lord GOD, Behold, I lay in **Zion** for a foundation a stone, a tried stone, a precious corner stone, a sure **foundation:** he that believeth shall not make haste. Isaiah 28:16

And the **city** had no need of the sun, neither of the moon, to shine in it: for the glory of God did lighten it, and the Lamb is the light thereof. Rev. 21:23

The Twelve Foundations of the Apostles

THE FOUNDATION OF THE SAINTS:

The <u>ROCK</u>, the Shepherd, the Stone, the Firm Foundation, the Lamb in the City, God within his people by the New Covenant in His Blood, the Light of the World, the Light of the City and the New Jerusalem

Precept 24: Parable of the Dragnet and the Judgment Written

> *"'Again, the kingdom of heaven is like a dragnet which was lowered into the sea, and gathered fish of every kind, and when it was full, they dragged it up on the beach; and they sat down and sorted out the good fish into baskets, but the worthless ones they threw away. So it will be at the end of the age; the angels will come and separate the wicked from the righteous and throw the wicked into the furnace of fire; in that place there will be weeping [over sorrow and pain] and grinding of teeth [over distress and anger]'" (Matthew 13:47-50 AMP).*

> *"**To execute on them the judgment written**. This is the honor for all His godly ones. Praise the Lord! (Hallelujah!)" (Psalm 149:9 AMP).*

Whatever is written in the Books of Moses, the Prophets and the Apostles concerning the wicked, that is their judgment. Nothing more, nothing less. For John wrote that it must be so. We are not to add to the words of the book nor take away from the words of the book.

> *"'I testify and warn everyone who hears the words of the prophecy of this book [its predictions, consolations, and ad-*

monitions]: if anyone adds [anything] to them, God will add to him the plagues (afflictions, calamities) which are written in this book; and if anyone takes away from or distorts the words of the book of this prophecy, God will take away [from that one] his share from the tree of life and from the holy city (new Jerusalem), which are written in this book'" (Revelation 22:18-19 AMP).

Precept 25: The Grace of Salvation: What must I do to be saved?

The Roman Road to Salvation

> "Well then, are we [Jews] better off than they? Not at all; for we have already charged that both Jews and Greeks (Gentiles) are under the control of sin and subject to its power. As it is written and forever remains written, 'There is none righteous [none that meets God's standard], not even one. There is none who understands, There is none who seeks for God. All have turned aside, together they have become useless; There is none who does good, no, not one; since all have sinned and continually fall short of the glory of God'" (Romans 3:9-12, 23 AMP).

> "For the wages of sin is death, but the free gift of God [that is, His remarkable, overwhelming gift of grace to believers] is eternal life in Christ Jesus our Lord" (Romans 6:23 AMP)

> "But God clearly shows and proves His own love for us, by the fact that while we were still sinners, Christ died for us" (Romans 5:8 AMP)

> "because if you acknowledge and confess with your mouth that Jesus is Lord [recognizing His power, authority, and majesty as God], and believe in your heart that God raised

Him from the dead, you will be saved. For with the heart a person believes [in Christ as Savior] resulting in his justification [that is, being made righteous—being freed of the guilt of sin and made acceptable to God]; and with the mouth he acknowledges and confesses [his faith openly], resulting in and confirming [his] salvation. For whoever calls on the name of the Lord [in prayer] will be saved" (Romans 10:9-10, 13 AMP)

"Therefore, since we have been justified [that is, acquitted of sin, declared blameless before God] by faith, [let us grasp the fact that] we have peace with God [and the joy of reconciliation with Him] through our Lord Jesus Christ (the Messiah, the Anointed)" (Romans 5:1 AMP).

"Therefore there is now no condemnation [no guilty verdict, no punishment] for those who are in Christ Jesus [who believe in Him as personal Lord and Savior]" (Romans 8:1 AMP).

"For I am convinced [and continue to be convinced—beyond any doubt] that neither death, nor life, nor angels, nor principalities, nor things present and threatening, nor things to come, nor powers, nor height, nor depth, nor any other created thing, will be able to separate us from the [unlimited] love of God, which is in Christ Jesus our Lord" (Romans 8:38-39 AMP).

Two ways to know

In the Spanish language there are two words that mean *to know. Saber* means to know facts and information, data, or how to do something such as a particular skill. The other word, *conocer,* means to know personally, to have personal knowledge of (in a relationship) relating to a person or a place. Some people claim to be Christian, but only "know" the facts of their religion. To know Jesus in the sense of walking by the Spirit He gave us (*conocer*), is something entirely different. He seeks to know us, intimately, in our hearts, by His Holy Spirit. If He speaks to you, draw near to Him and ask Him for forgiveness. Do not harden your heart.

Precept 26: To the Victorious and who partake of the Hidden Manna

♬ Pause and listen to *End of the Age: Book Two, "Strength for the Harvest."*
♬

Select scripture from Jeremiah and Revelation for your edification:

"'But they shall serve the Lord their God and [the descendant of] David their King, whom I will raise up for them'" (Jeremiah 30:9 AMP).

"Whoever has ears, let them hear what the Spirit says to the churches. To the one who is victorious, I will give the right to eat from the tree of life, which is in the paradise of God" (Revelation 2:7 AMP).

"Whoever has ears, let them hear what the Spirit says to the churches. The one who is victorious will not be hurt at all by the second death" (Revelation 2:11 AMP).

"Whoever has ears, let them hear what the Spirit says to the churches. To the one who is victorious, I will give some of the hidden manna. I will also give that person a white stone with a new name written on it, known only to the one who receives it" (Revelation 2:17 AMP).

"To the one who is victorious and does my will to the end, I will give authority over the nations" (Revelation 2:26 AMP).

"To the one who is victorious, I will give the right to sit with me on my throne, just as I was victorious and sat down with my Father on his throne" (Revelation 3:21 AMP).

"When the Lord brought back the captives to Zion (Jerusalem), We were like those who dream [it seemed so unreal]. Then our mouth was filled with laughter And our tongue with joyful shouting; Then they said among the nations,' The Lord has done great things for them. The Lord has done great things for us; We are glad! Restore our captivity, O Lord, As the streambeds in the South (the Negev) [are restored by torrents of rain]. They who sow in tears shall reap with joyful singing. He who goes back and forth weeping, carrying his bag of seed [for planting], Will indeed come again with a shout of joy, bringing his sheaves with him'" (Psalm 126:1-6 AMP).

"Do you not know? Have you not heard? The Everlasting God, the Lord, the Creator of the ends of the earth Does not become tired or grow weary; There is no searching of His understanding. He gives strength to the weary, And to him who has no might He increases power. Even youths grow weary and tired, And vigorous young men stumble badly, But those who wait for the Lord [who expect, look for, and hope in Him] Will gain new strength and renew their power; They will lift up their wings [and rise up close to God] like eagles [rising toward the sun]; They will run and not become weary, They will walk and not grow tired" (Isaiah 40:28-31 AMP).

♫ **Pause and listen to *End of the Age: Book Four, "Like Eagles Fly."*** ♫

"His breath is like an overflowing river, Which reaches to the neck, To sift the nations back and forth in a sieve [of disaster], And to put in the jaws of the peoples the bridle which leads to ruin. You will have a song as in the night when a holy feast is kept, And joy of heart as when one

marches [in procession] with a flute, To go to the [temple on the] mountain of the Lord, to the Rock of Israel. And the Lord will make His majestic voice heard, And show the descending of His arm [striking] in [His] fierce anger, And in the flame of a devouring fire, In the crashing sound of heavy rain, cloudburst, and hailstones" (Isaiah 30:28-30 AMP).

"Then the lame will leap like a deer, And the tongue of the mute will shout for joy. For waters will break forth in the wilderness And streams in the desert" (Isaiah 35:6 AMP).

"I kept looking Until thrones were set up, And the Ancient of Days (God) took His seat; His garment was white as snow And the hair of His head like pure wool. His throne was flames of fire; Its wheels were a burning fire. A river of fire was flowing And coming out from before Him; A thousand thousands were attending Him, And ten thousand times ten thousand were standing before Him; The court was seated, And the books were opened. Then I kept looking because of the sound of the great and boastful words which the horn was speaking. I kept looking until the beast was slain, and its body destroyed and given to be burned with fire" (Daniel 7:9-11 AMP).

The *fire* is the Word of God

"He said to them, 'The mystery of the kingdom of God has been given to you [who have teachable hearts], but those who are outside [the unbelievers, the spiritually blind] get everything in parables'" (Mark 4:11).

"Do not be afraid and anxious, little flock, for it is your Father's good pleasure to give you the kingdom" (Luke 12:32 NASB).

"It is the glory of God to conceal a matter, But the glory of kings is to search out a matter. As the heavens for height and the earth for depth, So the hearts and minds of kings are unsearchable" (Proverbs 25:23 AMP).

"He brought me up out of a horrible pit [of tumult and of

destruction], out of the miry clay, And He set my feet upon a rock, steadying my footsteps and establishing my path. He put a new song in my mouth, a song of praise to our God; Many will see and fear [with great reverence] And will trust confidently in the Lord. Blessed [fortunate, prosperous, and favored by God] is the man who makes the Lord his trust, And does not regard the proud nor those who lapse into lies (Psalm 40:24 AMP).

"O sing to the Lord a new song; Sing to the Lord, all the earth! Sing to the Lord, bless His name; Proclaim good news of His salvation from day to day. Declare His glory among the nations, His marvelous works and wonderful deeds among all the peoples" (Psalm 96:13 AMP).

"The Lord reigns, let the earth rejoice; Let the many islands and coastlands be glad. Clouds and thick darkness surround Him [as at Sinai]; Righteousness and justice are the foundation of His throne. Fire goes before Him And burns up His adversaries on all sides (Psalm 97:13 AMP)

"'Indeed, the former things have come to pass, Now I declare new things; Before they spring forth I proclaim them to you. Sing to the Lord a new song, Sing His praise from the end of the earth! You who go down to the sea, and all that is in it, You islands and coastlands, and those who inhabit them [sing His praise]! Let the wilderness and its cities lift up their voices, The villages where Kedar lives. Let the inhabitants of Sela shout for joy, Let them shout joyfully from the tops of the mountains'" (Isaiah 42:9-11 AMP).

"And I heard a voice from heaven, like the sound of great waters and like the rumbling of mighty thunder; and the voice that I heard [seemed like music and] was like the sound of harpists playing on their harps. And they sang a new song before the throne [of God] and before the four living creatures and the elders; and no one could learn the song except the hundred and forty-four thousand who had been purchased (ransomed, redeemed) from the earth. These are the ones who have not been defiled [by relations] with women, for they are celibate. These are the ones who follow the Lamb wherever He goes. These have been purchased and redeemed from among men [of Israel] as the first fruits [sanctified and set apart for special service] for God and the Lamb" (Revelation 14:24 AMP).

I was in a worship service once years ago and I the great waters and the rumbling of mighty thunder in my heart and spirit. It shook me to the core. I wept as I felt the presence of God.

> *"My mouth will speak wisdom, And the meditation of my heart will be understanding. I will incline my ear and consent to a proverb; On the lyre I will unfold my riddle. Why should I fear in the days of evil, When the wickedness of those who would betray me surrounds me [on every side]"* (Psalm 49:3-5 AMP)

> *"Again I looked, and this is what I saw: a white cloud, and sitting on the cloud was One like the Son of Man, with a crown of gold on His head and a sharp sickle [of swift judgment] in His hand. And another angel came out of the temple, calling with a loud voice to Him who was sitting upon the cloud, "Put in Your sickle and reap [at once], for the hour to reap [in judgment] has arrived, because the earth's harvest is fully ripened"* (Revelation 14:14-15).

Just as the sword of the Spirit is the Word of God, so is the sharp sickle of swift judgment the word of God, specifically prepared for the wicked. It will be a small book with open secrets and judgments from the books specifically selected and applicable for the wicked.

Everyone will know the Lord

> *"'And each man will no longer teach his neighbor and his brother, saying, 'Know the Lord,' for they will all know Me [through personal experience], from the least of them to the greatest,' says the Lord. 'For I will forgive their wickedness, and I will no longer remember their sin'"* (Jeremiah 31:34 AMP).

> *"But [the time is coming when] the earth shall be filled With the knowledge of the glory of the Lord, As the waters cover the sea"* (Habakkuk 2:14).

> *"Surely the Lord God does nothing Without revealing His secret plan [of the judgment to come] To His servants the*

prophets" (Amos 3:7).

"All things have been handed over to Me by My Father; and no one fully knows and accurately understands the Son except the Father; and no one fully knows and accurately understands the Father except the Son, and anyone to whom the Son [deliberately] wills to reveal Him" (Matthew 11:27).

"Then the disciples came to Him and asked, 'Why do You speak to the crowds in parables?' Jesus replied to them, 'To you it has been granted to know the mysteries of the kingdom of heaven, but to them it has not been granted. For whoever has [spiritual wisdom because he is receptive to God's word], to him more will be given, and he will be richly and abundantly supplied; but whoever does not have [spiritual wisdom because he has devalued God's word], even what he has will be taken away from him. This is the reason I speak to the crowds in parables: because while [having the power of] seeing they do not see, and while [having the power of] hearing they do not hear, nor do they understand and grasp [spiritual things]. In them the prophecy of Isaiah is being fulfilled, which says, 'You will hear and keep on hearing, but never understand; And you will look and keep on looking, but never comprehend; For this nation's heart has grown hard, And with their ears they hardly hear, And they have [tightly] closed their eyes, Otherwise they would see with their eyes, And hear with their ears, And understand with their heart, and turn [to Me] And I would heal them [spiritually].' 'But blessed [spiritually aware, and favored by God] are your eyes, because they see; and your ears, because they hear. I assure you and most solemnly say to you, many prophets and righteous men [who were honorable and in right standing with God] longed to see what you see, and did not see it, and to hear what you hear, and did not hear it'" (Matthew 13:10-17).

"For this reason, since the day we heard about it, we have not stopped praying for you, asking [specifically] that you may be filled with the knowledge of His will in all spiritual wisdom [with insight into His purposes], and in understanding [of spiritual things], so that you will walk in a manner worthy of the Lord [displaying admirable character, moral courage, and personal integrity], to [fully] please Him in all things, bearing fruit in every good work and steadily

growing in the knowledge of God [with deeper faith, clearer insight and fervent love for His precepts]" (Colossians 1:9-10).

"And He will judge between many peoples And render decisions for strong and distant nations. Then they shall hammer their swords into plowshares And their spears into pruning hooks [so that the implements of war may become the tools of agriculture]; Nation shall not lift up sword against nation, Nor shall they ever again train for war. Each of them shall sit [in security and peace] under his vine And under his fig tree, With no one to make them afraid, For the mouth of the [omnipotent] Lord of hosts has spoken it. For all the peoples [now] walk Each in the name of his god [in a transient relationship], As for us, we shall walk [securely]In the name of the Lord our [true] God forever and ever" (Micah 4:3-5 AMP).

"Now as they were eating Jesus took bread, and after blessing it, He broke it and gave it to the disciples, and said, 'Take, eat; this is My body.' And when He had taken a cup and given thanks, He gave it to them, saying, 'Drink from it, all of you'" (Matthew 26:25-27 AMP).

In the wedding feast, the bride and groom are seated on chairs and raised upon the shoulders of the people and paraded around the room during the banquet. We "meet our Lord in the air" in the banquet and are seated on thrones in the earth. Rise up in us Lord Jesus, Redeemer of us all. Glory to your Name. For your ways are higher than our ways and past finding out. Praise be to our LORD God who is above all gods.

The final section of this book will cite several pages in scripture that concern the wicked in the earth. They will serve you to begin tying up the judgments written against the wicked for legal persuasion —for since we swear on the Bible in court and the God of the Bible is printed on our currency, we should also be able to use His words in court. The appointed time for that event approaches (Daniel 7:26-27; Revelation 20:4a).

Remember that the overarching prophecy of the kingdom promised to the saints began in Genesis and is not fulfilled until the "end of the age." So, the fullness of the kingdom promises for the righteous come true at a specific time. The same is true of the kingdom actions and judgments upon the wicked—they also come to their fullness at a specific time, also the end of the age. If there ever was a great Sting Operation, this is it.

> *"And then I saw thrones, and sitting on them were those to whom judgment [that is, the authority to act as judges] was given" (Revelation 20:4a AMP).*

The kingdom yoke is light because God has already done all the heavy lifting. We believed His Word. The Wicked did not believe. All comes true. We inherit the truth of the fire of God's word. The works of the wicked are burned up. The works of the righteous withstand the test of the fire.

Many witnesses

I have brought multiple witnesses to bear in this book. The witnesses of scripture on any one topic listed here are multiple and agree together.

> *"But if he does not listen, take along with you one or two others, so that every word may be confirmed by the testimony of two or three witnesses" (Matthew 18:16 AMP).*
>
> *"And though one can overpower him who is alone, two can resist him. A cord of three strands is not quickly broken" (Ecclesiastes 4:12 AMP).*
>
> *"Do not be overcome and conquered by evil, but overcome evil with good" (Romans 12:21 AMP).*
>
> *"There is no fear in love [dread does not exist]. But perfect (complete, full grown) love drives out fear, because fear involves [the expectation of divine] punishment, so the one who is afraid [of God's judgment] is not perfected in love [has not grown into a sufficient understanding of God's love]" (1 John 4:18 AMP).*

The day of our Lord's vindication, and ours with His, is fast approaching. I need your help by sharing this book and preparing for the day of reckoning for the wicked outlined in "Operation Dragnet" below.

No weapon formed against you will succeed

"No weapon that is formed against you will succeed; And every tongue that rises against you in judgment you will condemn. This [peace, righteousness, security, and triumph over opposition] is the heritage of the servants of the LORD, And this is their vindication from Me,' says the LORD" (Isaiah 54:17 AMP).

Precept 27: Operation Dragnet

♫ Pause and listen to *End of the Age: Book Two, "The Dragnet."* ♫

Bitterness

Festering bitterness throughout history between nations addressed with conventional weapons has never worked. Man's diplomacy has failed. Only mutual respect, forgiveness and humility at the foot of the cross can bring peace. Those who refuse to...well, scripture is clear on that too (1 Peter 2:6-8).

So how did Jesus respond to betrayal? He washed Judas' feet (John 13). Scripture is clear as to how we should initially approach our enemies...until the Harvest and Dragnet.

The Sharp Sickle of Judgment and the Book of the Wicked

Open the books and see and understand their secrets for yourself. The judgments of the Bible contain all that is required to judge the wicked. This is the great dragnet prophesied by Jesus. The overarching prophecies of the kingdom of heaven speak of the "end," They were not only relevant in the time they were spoken, but also specifically and especially for the time of the end as we have seen.

And this is how it shall be

> "'At that time two men will be in the field; one will be taken [for judgment] and one will be left'" (Matthew 24:40 AMP).

133

Shaking of the nations and lack of restraint throughout the world

The nations and the world are now shaking like never before. There are earthquakes, wars and rumors of wars on all sides yet we were told the end was yet to come (Matthew 24:6). Many are concerned and greatly perplexed. But we have this promise:

> "His voice shook the earth [at Mount Sinai] then, but now He has given a promise, saying, "Yet once more I will shake not only the earth, but also the [starry] heaven." Now this [expression], "Yet once more," indicates the removal and final transformation of all those things which can be shaken—that is, of that which has been created—so that those things which cannot be shaken may remain" (Hebrews 12:26-27 AMP).

> "Where there is no vision [no revelation of God and His word], the people are unrestrained; But happy and blessed is he who keeps the law [of God]" (Proverbs 29:18 AMP).

It is up to the laborers of the harvest to publish the banner of the kingdom concerning the wicked and the righteous in this hour.

God's covenant with Abraham is established forever

> "O you offspring of Abraham, His servant, O you sons of Jacob, His chosen ones! He is the Lord our God; His judgments are in all the earth. He has remembered His covenant forever, The word which He commanded and established to a thousand generations, The covenant which He made with Abraham, And His sworn oath to Isaac, Which He confirmed to Jacob as a statute, To Israel as an everlasting covenant, Saying, 'To you I will give the land of Canaan As the measured portion of your inheritance.' When there were only a few men in number, Very few [in fact], and strangers in it; And they wandered from one nation to another, From one kingdom to another people, He allowed no man to oppress them; He rebuked kings for their sakes, saying, 'Do not touch My anointed ones, And do My prophets no harm'" (Psalm 105:6-15 AMP).

God's Word is established in heaven forever and cannot be shaken

The people of the nations are unrestrained and wickedness abounds just as Paul told Timothy. Take heart. The reading of this book will encourage you. The process of writing it has taken me on a journey of over two decades. It has cost me dearly. But we must remember that the Father is the chief vine dresser. He prunes us so that we will bear much fruit (John 15). He also sets the seasons and times for when we will bear that fruit. That season for me is arriving. Join with me now in uniting the Body of Christ. Gather and prepare to cast the great dragnet.

"Forever, O Lord, Your word is settled in heaven [standing firm and unchangeable]" (Psalm 119:89 AMP).

Meaningless arguments in the city gate (courts)

"Those who cause a person to be condemned with a [false] word, And lay a trap for him who upholds justice at the [city] gate, And defraud the one in the right with meaningless arguments. Therefore, the Lord, who redeemed Abraham [from paganism] says this, concerning the house of Jacob (Israel): Jacob will not be ashamed, nor will his face turn pale [with disappointment because of his children's degenerate behavior]; For when he sees his children, the work of My hands, in his midst, They will sanctify My Name; They will sanctify the Holy One of Jacob And will stand in awe and reverent fear of the God of Israel. "Those who err in mind will know the truth, And those who criticize and murmur discontentedly will accept instruction" (Isaiah 29:21-24 AMP).

Judges and officers in the city gates must judge righteously

"Every man shall give as he is able, in accordance with the blessing which the Lord your God has given you. You shall appoint judges and officers in all your cities (gates) which the Lord your God is giving you, according to your tribes, and they shall judge the people with righteous judgment.

135

You shall not distort justice; you shall not be partial, and you shall not take a bribe, for a bribe blinds the eyes of the wise and perverts the words of the righteous" (Deuteronomy 16:17-19).

Scripture descriptions of the wicked

Begin to publish these and quotes from the passages online on the web after you have established a good study group regarding the precepts in this book.

"Now the practices of the sinful nature are clearly evident: they are sexual immorality, impurity, sensuality (total ir-responsibility, lack of self control), idolatry, sorcery, hostility, strife, jealousy, fits of anger, disputes, dissensions, factions [that promote heresies], envy, drunkenness, riotous behavior, and other things like these. I warn you beforehand, just as I did previously, that those who practice such things will not inherit the kingdom of God" (Galatians 5:19-21 AMP).

"For [God does not overlook sin and] the wrath of God is revealed from heaven against all ungodliness and un-righteousness of men who in their wickedness suppress and stifle the truth, because that which is known about God is evident within them [in their inner consciousness], for God made it evident to them. For ever since the creation of the world His invisible attributes, His eternal power and divine nature, have been clearly seen, being understood through His workmanship [all His creation, the wonderful things that He has made], so that they [who fail to believe and trust in Him] are without excuse and without defense. For even though they knew God [as the Creator], they did not honor Him as God or give thanks [for His wondrous creation]. On the contrary, they became worthless in their thinking [godless, with pointless reasonings, and silly speculations], and their foolish heart was darkened. Claiming to be wise, they became fools, and exchanged the glory and majesty and excellence of the immortal God for an image [worthless idols] in the shape of mortal man and birds and fourfooted animals and reptiles. Therefore God gave them over in the lusts of their own hearts to [sexual] impurity, so that their bodies would be dishonored among them [abandoning

them to the degrading power of sin], because [by choice] they exchanged the truth of God for a lie, and worshiped and served the creature rather than the Creator, who is blessed forever! Amen. For this reason God gave them over to degrading and vile passions; for their women exchanged the natural function for that which is unnatural [a function contrary to nature], and in the same way also the men turned away from the natural function of the woman and were consumed with their desire toward one another, men with men committing shameful acts and in return receiving in their own bodies the inevitable and appropriate penalty for their wrongdoing. And since they did not see fit to acknowledge God or consider Him worth knowing [as their Creator], God gave them over to a depraved mind, to do things which are improper and repulsive, until they were filled (permeated, saturated) with every kind of unrighteousness, wickedness, greed, evil; full of envy, murder, strife, deceit, malice and meanspiritedness . They are gossips [spreading rumors], slanderers, haters o f God, insolent, arrogant, boastful, inventors [of new forms] o f evil, disobedient and disrespectful to parents, without understanding, untrustworthy, unloving, unmerciful [withou t pity]. Although they know God's righteous decree and Hi s judgment, that those who do such things deserve death, yet the y not only do them, but they even [enthusiastically] approv e and tolerate others who practice them"
(Romans 1:18-32 AMP).

"But understand this, that in the last days dangerous times [of great stress and trouble] will come [difficult days that will be hard to bear]. For people will be lovers of self [narcissistic, self-focused], lovers of money [impelled by greed], boastful, arrogant, revilers, disobedient to parents, ungrateful, unholy and profane, [and they will be] unloving [devoid of natural human affection, calloused and inhumane], irreconcilable, malicious gossips, devoid of self control [intemperate, immoral], brutal, haters of good, traitors, reckless , conceited, lovers of [sensual] pleasure rather than lovers o f God, holding to a form of [outward] godliness (religion) , although they have denied its power [for their conduc t nullifies their claim of faith]. Avoid such people and keep fa r away from them. For among them are those who worm thei r way into homes and captivate morally weak and spiritual ly dwarfed women weighed down by [the burden of thei r] sins, easily swayed by various impulses, always learning a nd listening to anybody who will teach them, but never able

to come to the knowledge of the truth. Just as Jannes and Jambr es [the court magicians of Egypt] opposed Moses, so these m en also oppose the truth, men of depraved mind, unqualified a nd worthless [as teachers] in regard to the faith. But they wi ll not get very far, for their meaningless nonsense and ignoran ce will become obvious to everyone, as was that of Jannes a nd Jambres" (2 Timothy 3:19 AMP).

The foolish

"Nevertheless in the same way, these dreamers [who are dreaming that God will not punish them] also defile the body, and reject [legitimate] authority, and revile and mock angelic majesties. But even the archangel Michael, when he was disputing with the devil (Satan), and arguing about the body of Moses, did not dare bring an abusive condemnation against him, but [simply] said, "The Lord rebuke you!" But these men sneer at anything which they do not understand; and whatever they do know by [mere] instinct, like unreasoning and irrational beasts—by these things they are destroyed. Woe to them! For they have gone the [defiant] way of Cain, and for profit they have run headlong into the error of Balaam, and perished in the rebellion of [mutinous] Korah. These men are hidden reefs [elements of great danger to others] in your love feasts when they feast together with you without fear, looking after [only] themselves; [they are like] clouds without water, swept along by the winds; autumn trees without fruit, doubly dead, uprooted and lifeless; wild waves of the sea, flinging up their own shame like foam; wandering stars, for whom the gloom of deep darkness has been reserved forever. It was about these people that Enoch, in the seventh generation from Adam, prophesied, when he said, "Look, the Lord came with myriads of His holy ones to execute judgment upon all, and to convict all the ungodly of all the ungodly deeds they have done in an ungodly way, and of all the harsh and cruel things ungodly sinners have spoken against Him." These people are [habitual] murmurers, griping and complaining, following after their own desires [controlled by passion]; they speak arrogantly, [pretending admiration and] flattering people to gain an advantage. But as for you, beloved, remember the [prophetic] words

spoken by the apostles of our Lord Jesus Christ. They used to say to you, "In the last days there will be scoffers, following after their own ungodly passions." These are the ones who are [agitators] causing divisions—worldlyminded [secular, unspiritual, carnal, merely sensual—unsaved], devoid of the Spirit. But you, beloved, build yourselves up on [the foundation of] your most holy faith [continually progress, rise like an edifice higher and higher], pray in the Holy Spirit, and keep yourselves in the love of God, waiting anxiously and looking forward to the mercy of our Lord Jesus Christ [which will bring you] to eternal life. And have mercy on some, who are doubting; save others, snatching them out of the fire; and on some have mercy but with fear, loathing even the clothing spotted and polluted by their shameless immoral freedom. Now to Him who is able to keep you from stumbling or falling into sin, and to present you unblemished [blameless and faultless] in the presence of His glory with triumphant joy and unspeakable delight, to the only God our Savior, through Jesus Christ our Lord, be glory, majesty, dominion, and power, before all time and now and forever. Amen" (Jude 1:825 AMP).

"Their [wicked, godless] judges are thrown down the sides of the rocky cliff, And they [who followed them] will hear my words, for they are pleasant (just)" (Psalm 141:6 AMP).

The effect of bribes on justice and vision

The word "bribe(s)" occurs twenty-nine times in the Bible. It is closely connected to the perversion of justice and vision and immoral control of others or governance. I will share a few verses here:

"You shall not accept a bribe, for a bribe blinds the clear-sighted and subverts the testimony and the cause of the righteous" (Exodus 23:8 AMP).

"'Cursed is he who accepts a bribe to strike down an innocent person.' And all the people shall say, 'Amen.'" (Deuteronomy 27:25 (AMP)

They must be denounced openly.

"Therefore you have no excuse or justification, every one of you who [hypocritically] judges and condemns others; for in passing judgment on another person, you condemn yourself, because you who judge [from a position of arrogance or self-righteousness] are habitually practicing the very same things [which you denounce]" (Romans 2:1 AMP).

"On the contrary, it is you who wrong and defraud, and you do this even to your brothers and sisters. Do you not know that the unrighteous will not inherit or have any share in the kingdom of God? Do not be deceived; neither the sexually immoral, nor idolaters, nor adulterers, nor effeminate [by perversion], nor those who participate in homosexuality, nor thieves, nor the greedy, nor drunkards, nor revilers [whose words are used as weapons to abuse, insult, humiliate, intimidate, or slander], nor swindlers will inherit or have any share in the kingdom of God" (1 Corinthians 6:8-10 AMP).

"Men will say, 'Surely there is a reward for the righteous; Surely there is a God who judges on the earth'" (Psalm 58:11 AMP).

"The Lord laughs at him [the wicked one—the one who oppresses the righteous], For He sees that his day [of defeat] is coming" (Psalm 37:13 AMP).

"The Lord executes righteousness And justice for all the oppressed" (Psalm 103:6 AMP).

"If you see the oppression of the poor and the denial of justice and righteousness in the province, do not be shocked at the sight [of corruption]; for a higher official watches over another official, and there are higher ones over them [looking out for one another]" (Ecclesiastes 5:8 AMP).

"For the vineyard of the Lord of hosts is the house (nation) of Israel And the men of Judah are His delightful planting [which He loves]. So He looked for justice, but in fact, [He saw] bloodshed and lawlessness; [He looked] for righteousness, but in fact, [He heard] a cry of distress and oppression" (Isaiah 5:7 AMP).

"They hatch vipers' eggs and weave the spider's webs;
He who eats of their eggs dies,
And from an egg which is crushed a viper breaks out.
Their webs will not serve as clothing,
Nor will they cover themselves with what they make;
Their works are works of wickedness [of sin, of injustice, of
wrongdoing],
And the act of violence is in their hands.
Their feet run to evil,
And they rush to shed innocent blood.
Their thoughts are thoughts of wickedness [of sin, of injus-
tice, of wrongdoing];
Devastation and destruction are in their highways" (Isaiah
59:5-7 AMP).

"For look, the wicked are bending the bow; They take aim
with their arrow on the string To shoot [by stealth] in dark-
ness at the upright in heart"(Psalms 11:2 AMP).

Prophets stealing the words of other prophets

"'Therefore behold (hear this), I am against the [counter-
feit] prophets,' says the Lord, '[I am descending on them
with punishment, these prophets] who steal My words from
one another [imitating the words of the true prophets]'"
(Jeremiah 23:30 AMP).

Perjury, deception, murder, stealing and violence

"There is [false] swearing of oaths, deception (broken
faith), murder, stealing, and adultery; They employ violence, so that one [act of] bloodshed follows closely on
another" (Hosea 4:2).

Time for judgment and reward

"The nations were angry, and your wrath has come. The

141

time has come for judging the dead, and for rewarding your
servants the prophets and your people who revere your name,
both great and small—and for destroying those who destroy
the earth" (Revelation 11:18 AMP).

Who loses their authority to rule?

"Do you not know that the unrighteous will not inherit or
have any share in the kingdom of God? Do not be deceived;
neither the sexually immoral, nor idolaters, nor adulterers,
nor effeminate [by perversion], nor those who participate
in homosexuality, nor thieves, nor the greedy, nor drunk-
ards, no revilers [whose words are used as weapons to abuse,
insult, humiliate, intimidate, or slander], nor swindlers
will inherit or have any share in the kingdom of God" (1
Corinthians 6:9-10 AMP).

Publish the works of the wicked

Searchable terms in 1 Corinthians 6, Galatians 5, Jude 1 include many
of those shared here. To find more, search online at www.biblegateway
.com. Online Bibles permit you to search multiple languages so that the
judgements can be published (copied and pasted) in multiple languages
and published worldwide. Please choose Bible versions in the public
domain.

Officials, officers, mutter, wicked, wickedness, oppress, oppression, teal,
murder, unnatural affection, proud, own strength, trust in own might,
fleshly, lust, vain, foolish, lazy, idolatrous, worshiping idols, showing
favoritism, works of the flesh, worldly, judge, justice, just judges, judges
unjustly, injustice, judge wickedly, wicked judges, war, make war, oppress, oppress poor, poor, leaders, leader, accuse, make the righteous
a prey, prey on the righteous, fool, selfish, unholy, false accusations,
make the righteous a prey, prey on the upright, twist the truth, false
accusations, bribe and violence.

A brief outline includes:

    1. Evil Behavior/Sins
      - Murder (Genesis 9:5; Exodus 20:13; Numbers 35:16)
      - Adultery (Exodus 20:14; Leviticus 20:10; Proverbs 6:23;
      Matthew 5:28; Matthew 5:32; Matthew 19:9)

- Violence
- Theft (John 10:10; Exodus 20:15; Exodus 22:1; Leviticus 19:11)
- Idolatry (Numbers 31:3; Exodus 34:1; Judges 3; 1 Samuel 15:23; Isaiah 44:9; Jeremiah 3:8; Hosea 6:10; 1 Corinthians 10:14; Galatians 5:20; Colossians 3:5; Revelation 19:2 [adultery=idolatry]).
- Coveting (Exodus 20:17; Exodus 34:24; Deuteronomy 5:21; Deuteronomy 7:25; Joshua 6:18; Proverbs 16:29; Micah 2:2; Mark 7:22; Luke 12; Romans 7:7-8; Romans 13:9; James 4:2).
- Lying *"A lying tongue hates those it wounds and crushes, And a flattering mouth works ruin" (Proverbs 26:28 AMP).*
- Pride *"Pride goes before destruction, And a haughty spirit before a fall" (Proverbs 16:18 AMP).*
- Oppression of the poor and vulnerable *"He who oppresses the poor taunts and insults his Maker, But he who is kind and merciful and gracious to the needy honors Him" (Proverbs 14:31 AMP).*

2. Immoral Acts
- Sexual immorality (Ezekiel 16:25-29; Matthew 5:32; Matthew 19:9; 1 Corinthians 5:1; 1 Corinthians 6:13-18; 1 Corinthians 7:2; 1 Corinthians 10:8; 2 Corinthians 12:21; Galatians 5:19).
- Injustice/bribe(s) (2 Chronicles 19:7; Job 15:34; *"...gave Pul a thousand talents of silver [as a bribe], so that he might help him to strengthen his control of the kingdom" (2 Kings 15:19b AMP).*
- Exploitation (2 Peter 2:3; Leviticus 19:13)
- Deception (2 Thessalonians 2:3; Deuteronomy 11:16)

3. Judicial Error
- Unjust (Deuteronomy 25:16; 2 Chronicles 19:7; Proverbs 43:1; Proverbs 16:10; Proverbs 20:21; Proverbs 28:16)
- False witness or report (Exodus 23:1; Deuteronomy 19:16; Deuteronomy 19:18; Proverbs 6:19; Proverbs 12:17; Proverbs 14:5; Proverbs 19:5-9; Proverbs 21:28)

Acknowledgments

♫ Pause and listen to *End of the Age: Book Three, "Lori's Song."* ♫

To my adoring crown, whose burning anger has kept me safe from speaking God's words out of season, many thanks are due you—not only from me, but from those who shall believe because of this message.

Use the same net the wicked have prepared

> *"The nations have sunk down in the pit which they have made; In the net which they hid, their own foot has been caught" Psalm 9:15 AMP).*

> *They set a net for my steps; My very life was bowed down. They dug a pit before me; Into the midst of it they themselves have fallen. Selah" (Psalm 57:6 AMP).*

> *"Let the wicked fall into their own nets, While I pass by and safely escape [from danger]" (Psalm 141:10 AMP).*

> *"The violence of the wicked will [return to them and] drag them away [like fish caught in a net], Because they refuse to act with justice" (Proverbs 21:7 AMP).*

> *The godly person [who is faithful and loyal to God] has perished from the earth, And there is no upright person [one with good character and moral integrity] among men. They all lie in wait to shed blood; Each hunts the other with a net" (Micah 7:2 AMP).*

The Dragnet

> *"'Again, the kingdom of heaven is like a dragnet which was lowered into the sea, and gathered fish of every kind, and when it was full, they dragged it up on the beach; and they sat down and sorted out the good fish into baskets, but the worthless ones they threw away. So it will be at the end of the age; the angels will come and separate the wicked from the righteous and throw the wicked into the furnace of fire; in that place there will be weeping [over sorrow and pain] and grinding of teeth [over distress and anger]'" (Matthew 13:47-50 AMP).*

You have a great part to play

The wicked will ultimately lose their authority as they are labeled with scriptures of wickedness.

> *"When the righteous are in authority and become great, the people rejoice; But when the wicked man rules, the people groan and sigh" (Proverbs 29:2 AMP).*

> *"If a ruler pays attention to lies [and encourages corruption], All his officials will become wicked" (Proverbs 29:12 AMP).*

This is our inheritance. This is the renewal when Jesus Christ the Morning Star rises in our hearts and is glorified in the Earth. It is when the fire of the judgment promised begins to burn in the earth. God's Word will consume the dead works of the wicked. The righteous will rise and inherit the thrones of the land. Peace will grow and not cease.

> *"But the Scripture has imprisoned everyone [everything—the entire world] under sin, so that [the inheritance, the blessing of salvation] which was promised through faith in Jesus Christ might be given to those who believe [in Him and acknowledge Him as God's precious Son]" (Galatians 3:22 AMP).*

"I in them and You in Me, that they may be perfected and completed into one, so that the world may know [without any doubt] that You sent Me, and [that You] have loved them, just as You have loved Me" (John 17:23 AMP).

When? I believe it is now: "There will be no more delay" (Rev. 10). All the works of the wicked must be finished. Then we bind the wicked with the Word which is a consuming fire. Meanwhile, and always, persuade the rest with gentleness and tears to reach out to Jesus Christ for salvation.

"Jesus said to him, 'I am the [only] Way [to God] and the [real] Truth and the [real] Life; no one comes to the Father but through Me'" (John 14:6 AMP).

"'I say to you, whoever declares openly and confesses Me before men [speaking freely of Me as his Lord], the Son of Man also will declare openly and confess him [as one of His own] before the angels of God. But he who denies Me before men will be denied in the presence of the angels of God. And everyone who speaks a word against the Son of Man, it will be forgiven him; but he who blasphemes against the Holy Spirit [that is, whoever intentionally discredits the Holy Spirit by attributing the authenticating miracles done by Me to Satan], it will not be forgiven him [for him there is no forgiveness]. When they bring you before the synagogues and the magistrates and the authorities, do not be worried about how you are to defend yourselves or what you are to say; for the Holy Spirit will teach you in that very hour what you ought to say'" (Luke 12:8-12 AMP).

To the many who have misunderstood me—close family, not so close friends and those close alike. Forgive me if the message contained here caused me to faint and act strangely around you, for as the prophet Daniel was weak and lost all his strength when the Lord spoke to him, so it has been with me at times. And ultimately, to the Lord, keeper of all the keys of our understanding: may He enlighten all who read this book as He has taught me. Bring along our side your Holy Spirit and great counselors as we seek to do your will in this hour of trouble. Let everything that has breath praise the Lord! Amen.

Where is my boasting?

🎵 Pause and listen to *End of the Age: Book One, "I Will Not Trust."* 🎵

> *"Thus says the LORD, 'Let not the one who is wise and skilled boast in his insight; let not the one who is mighty and powerful boast in his strength; let not the one who is rich boast in his [temporal satisfactions and earthly] abundance; but let the one who boasts boast in this, that he understands and knows Me [and acknowledges Me and honors Me as God and recognizes without any doubt], that I am the LORD who practices lovingkindness, justice and righteousness on the earth, for in these things I delight," says the LORD" (Jeremiah 9:23-24 AMP).*

This is my boast in the Lord who has taught me since I was a child to lean on Him and trust in Him.

A Word about the Word and a word about words

Words have always possessed at least two things: 1) creative power or 2) destructive power; they either edify or tear down.

> *"A soothing tongue [speaking words that build up and encourage] is a tree of life, but a perversive tongue [speaking words that overwhelm and depress] crushes the spirit" (Proverbs 15:4 AMP).*

> *"In the beginning [before all-time] was the Word (Christ), and the Word was with God, and the Word was God Himself. He was [continually existing] in the beginning [co-eternally] with God. All things were made and came into existence through Him; and without Him not even one thing was made that has come into being. In Him was life [and the power to bestow life], and the life was the Light of men. The Light shines on in the darkness, and the darkness did not understand it or overpower it or appropriate it or absorb it [and is unreceptive to it]" (John 1:1-5 AMP).*

> *"His mouth is full of curses and deceit [fraud] and oppres-*

sion; Under his tongue is mischief and wickedness [injustice and sin]" (Psalms 10:7 AMP).

"A time to tear apart and a time to sew together; A time to keep silent and a time to speak" (Ecclesiastes 3:7 AMP).

The time has come to speak. When we do speak, we must remember that judgment begins with the church just as Jesus was always rebuking the religious for their hypocrisy. Please consider what was spoken into my hearing only yesterday:

God judges those outside the church (non-Christians)

In all these things we must remember the example of Jesus' judgment. He was a friend to sinners and a constant rebuke to the hypocritical religious. He looked at the woman caught in adultery and did not condemn her, but called her to go and to sin no more. Neither do we condemn yet we must judge justly and say, "sin no more."

"Sooner or later, we sit down to a banquet of consequences."
Robert Louis Stevenson (Scottish novelist and poet 1850-1894)

"Surely this phrase 'the wrath of God' is greatly misunderstood. Many think, invariably, of some sort of peeved deity, a kind of cosmic, terrible-tempered Mr. Band, who indulges in violent, uncontrolled displays of temper when human beings do not do what they ought to do. But such a concept only reveals the limitations of our understanding. The Bible never deals with the wrath of God that way. According to Scriptures, the wrath of God is God's moral integrity. When man refuses to yield himself to God, he creates certain conditions, not only for himself but for others as well, which God has ordained for harm. It is God who makes evil result in sorrow, heartache, injustice, and despair. It is God's way of saying to man, 'Now look, you must face the truth. You were made for Me. If you decide that you don't want Me, then you will have to bear the consequences.' The absence of God is destructive to human life. That absence is God's wrath. And God cannot withhold it. In His moral

integrity, He insists that these things should occur as a result of our disobedience. He sets man's sin and His wrath in the same frame."
Charles R. Swindoll, Living Above the Level of Medioc-
rity (2016)

About the Author

♫ Pause and listen to *End of the Age: Book Three, "Chalice."* ♫

Chalice of suffering gives way to Chalice of Victory for the author

My parents divorced when I was around eight years old, an important age for a little boy. My dad, while an honorable man, was emotionally absent from me from time to time. That was the case, and I was also a quiet introvert that didn't seem to care or notice. Nonetheless, I was emotionally bruised and my soul developed an open tear of which the enemy of our souls took advantage. At the age of sixteen I looked in the mirror with a knife in my hand and considered taking my own life—an idea that clearly wasn't mine or God's (John 10:10). As you can see by now, I didn't take my own life and that was a good thing since I am now married and have two wonderful children, who like myself, have had their own spiritual and mental battles that they have overcome. As of November 2024 they have overcome many of their own personal battles and are serving the LORD to the best of the ability and serving their fellowman.

After graduating college in 1994, I was spiritually mentored by a man named James Forde who had written a gospel track titled *What is meant by Salvation?* Under his guidance and instruction, I learned some interesting details about the Great Commission and that *"in the name"* is not a stamp of approval. Rather, it is a legal act of adoption. In the Greek it is translated "baptized *into* the name." I am a part of His household. I had been baptized *into* the name of the Father, the Son and the Holy Spirit. What is His is also mine—and yours if you are also His. The life that is His is now mine. This truth is clearly explained in other scriptures but I had just not understood exactly until then. Shortly after that realization I was given a book, I don't remember from who, titled *Bondage Breaker* by Neil T. Anderson. He is the founder of Freedom in Christ Ministries[1] . Read the book and you will understand the truths in Paul's letter to the Ephesians that were applied to my life in order to be set free from my chalice of suffering.

One day in 1994 or 1995 while driving home, I felt some sensations inside my body like something was moving around inside of me. This occurred *after* I had learned about baptism *into* the name. *When* I arrived home I started praying. I suddenly realized that I was battling a spiritual enemy. I took a shower, got dressed and went to my mentor's print shop which was housed in a small business building in a nearby town. The events of the next two days were both horrifying and liberating. We battled demons of all kinds and cast them out of my flesh. Neil T. Anderson teaches the right way to do this with a Truth approach and does not permit them to speak. We were not familiar with this approach. Needless to say, at the end of the two days my body was very, very sore. Sometimes during the deliverance, the demons would speak through me. During one instance one of them identified himself as Chalice. I have tried to reflect on that recently and to what that meant. I was delivered from many demons during that event of which my fiancé was a witness. Did it mean he was assigned to me to call others with him and torment me? Perhaps. All I know is that my victory was only found in the authority of the name of Jesus Christ.

> *"And there is salvation in and through no one else, for there is no other name under heaven given among men by and in which we must be saved" (Acts 4:12 AMP).*

> *"For this reason also [because He obeyed and so completely humbled Himself], God has highly exalted Him and bestowed on Him the name which is above every name, so that at the name of Jesus every knee shall bow [in submission], of those who are in heaven and on earth and under the earth, and that every tongue will confess and openly acknowledge that Jesus Crist is Lord [sovereign God], to the glory of God the Father" (Philippians 2:9-11 AMP).*

A few years later, when I was teaching in a small school in the southwest

---

1. https://www.ficm.org

of the state, I had a student that said she had a spirit guide that she could see. It happened one day that she had finished her work early and I asked her about the book she was reading at her desk. She disclosed to me that it was a book about spirit guides. I said that kind of reading was dangerous. She said that she could see her spirit guide follow her around school but that it wouldn't come into my classroom. She also said that the spirit guide would be angry with her if she burned all her spirit guide books as I suggested.

In the book of James, we read that if we resist the devil and submit to God that the enemy will flee. But she was not a believer yet. So I loaned her my book by Neil T. Anderson, *The Bondage Breaker*. She read it, confessed aloud Jesus as her Savior to me, burned the books, and was set free. Glory be to God! Years later I learned that she continued to follow Christ from that day forward until now.

Looking back to the year 1998, when I felt the call of God on my life to teach and preach, I wrote my first song inspired by Psalm 51. Psalm 51 is a song of repentance. Even now I consider it to be an important part of my testimony, including Psalm 38:4,

> *"For my iniquities have gone over my head [like the waves of a flood]; As a heavy burden they weigh too much for me."*

Just as the apostle Paul shares, God has chosen the weak and foolish things of this world to shame those who think they are wise. I am not a strong man by any means. I have fallen into iniquity and been trapped by addictions, other than smoking and alcohol, more than once in my life. I had given up on this project and had set it aside for several months now thinking it would be a something I would never pick up again. But as you can see, God had other plans.

> *"Humble yourself under the mighty hand of God and He will exalt you in due time."*

This is not just my time; I share it with all believers around the world. It is time for the body of Christ to arise victorious and possess the gates where wickedness rules at every level.

Rembrandt painted himself into one of his Paintings of the Cru-

cifixion

One of my older brothers pointed out to me recently that in one of Rembrandt's renderings of the crucifixion of Jesus Christ, he painted his self-portrait at the foot of the cross looking up at the face of the Savior. Even Rembrandt understood his need for a Savior.

"Jesus said to him, 'I am the [only] Way [to God] and the [real] Truth and the [real] Life; no one comes to the Father but through Me'" (John 14:6 AMP).

"For whoever wishes to save his life [in this world] will [eventually] lose it [through death], but whoever loses his life [in this world] for My sake will find it [that is, life with Me for all eternity]" (Matthew 16:25 AMP).

"People will speak of the power of Your awesome acts, And [with gratitude and submissive wonder] will tell of Your greatness" (Psalms 145:6 AMP).

Prepare the words of judgment from the sacred texts. Post them and send them. Translate them and publish them. The world must burn with the fire of God's word.

The time has come.

A poignant question and some directions

Why do great nations spend billions on war and yet neglect the weak and poor? Upon this and more they will be judged. Follow the judgments written and publish them and the renewal will begin. Start with online groups to join and name them Operation Dragnet by City and Country. Prepare documents and posts with the selected scriptures most relevant for the wicked judges and officials for all levels of government and include officials' names. Do not add or subtract to what is written in the Word of God. Enlist leaders in each county seat to form a group and extend invitations to other churches in neighboring cities and all county seats. As your state begins to get saturated with prayer and study groups, share this book with those in prison. Love on them and share with them your own struggles. Volunteer. Love on and share this great vision with families that are dealing with hopelessness. For there is real hope. It is here. It is now. It is in our hands. We are His hands and feet. We must walk in love. Perfect love drives out fear. Perfect love overcomes the darkness and evil. It is time to overcome. It is time to no longer turn the other cheek. It is time to embrace the fight with the sword of truth.

Epilogue

Adam in the Garden and the Judgment

♫ Pause and listen to *End of the Age: Book Three, "First Commands."* ♫

As I was considering how to end this book I was reminded of something in the story of Adam in Genesis that is connected to the judgment in Revelation: namely the care of the earth. Consider the following:

> *"The LORD God took the human and settled him in the garden of Eden to farm it and to take care of it" (Genesis 2:15 CEB).*

It is not my place to argue as to whether or not this happened literally. However, I'm convinced that it is symbolic of one of the roles that God has for man in the earth. Other translations of this verse say that Adam was supposed to "tend," "cultivate," "keep," or "guard" the Garden of Eden. This was Adam's responsibility. This was a command. Now consider this phrase in Revelation regarding verse 11:18:

> *"...and [the time came] to destroy the destroyers of the earth" (AMP).*
>
> *"And He will judge between many peoples And render decisions for strong and distant nations. Then they shall hammer their swords into plowshares And their spears into*

157

*pruning hooks [so that the implements of war may become the tools of **agriculture**]; Nation shall not lift up sword against nation, or shall they ever again train for war" (Micah 4:3 AMP).*

Keeping and managing natural resources properly and cultivating the earth is a priority for man. It is part of his purpose because the earth sustains his physical life. The tree of the field and the fish of the sea are for the service of man—not for his exploitation. All natural resources should be managed wisely.

All buildings should be built as wisely as is reasonable. Those that destroy them mock the Creator, their builder and those that live in them. Another consideration is from the book of James:

"Pure and unblemished religion [as it is expressed in outward acts] in the sight of our God and Father is this: to visit and look after the fatherless and the widows in their distress, and to keep oneself uncontaminated by the [secular] world" (James 1:27 AMP).

Notice again, as I have said before that Genesis is connected to Revelation. In the case above, it was the earth. In the case of Abraham, it was the possession of the gates of his enemies by his descendants.

What about business dealings? Yes, there is a judgment for this as well:

"He who increases his wealth by interest and usury (excessive interest) Gathers it for him who is gracious to the poor. He who turns his ear away from listening to the law [of God and man], Even his prayer is repulsive [to God]" (Proverbs 28:8-9 AMP).

So where is condemnation?

There is a flipside to a popular verse that is seldom quoted in its full context. That verse is John 3:16. You have probably seen it on signs that have popped up at sporting events. The condemnation and judgment comes in the verses following John 3:16:

"For God so [greatly] loved and dearly prized the world, that He [even] gave His [One and] only begotten Son, so that whoever believes and trusts in Him [as Savior] shall not perish, but have eternal life. For God did not send the Son into the world to judge and condemn the world [that is, to initiate the final judgment of the world], but that the world might be saved through Him. Whoever believes and has decided to trust in Him [as personal Savior and Lord] is not judged [for this one, there is no judgment, no rejection, no condemnation]; **but the one who does not believe [and has decided to reject Him as personal Savior and Lord] is judged already [that one has been convicted and sentenced], because he has not believed and trusted in the name of the [One and] only begotten Son of God [the One who is truly unique, the only One of His kind, the One who alone can save him]"** *(John 3:16-18 AMP).*

"But the one who denies and rejects Me before men, **that one I will also deny and reject** *before My Father who is in heaven" (Matthew 10:33 AMP).*

"But when the Son of Man comes in His glory and majesty and all the angels with Him, then He will sit on the throne of His glory. All the nations will be gathered before Him [for judgment]; and He will separate them from one another, as a shepherd separates his sheep from the goats; and He will put the sheep on His right [the place of honor], **and the goats on His left [the place of rejection]"** *(Matthew 25:31-33 AMP).*

Final Thoughts

Throughout this book I have shared multiple songs that hopefully have inspired, instructed and caused spiritual truths buried deep in your spirit to come alive. It is my wish that they might remind you of what you read so that referencing the book often might be unnecessary and that you would be able to pass the book on to someone else. If you can share multiple books with others and sow "many seeds," all the better.

Since this is a *Study Guide*, it is up to you to look up any references. In this modern age we have many resources at our disposal to do that quickly. Use what you like. I prefer the Amplified Bible.

End of the Age: Book Five

Book Five, the final music album of the series, depicts the three heirs to the Messianic Promise of Blessing on the cover: Abraham, Isaac and Jacob.

> *"I say to you that there are many [Gentiles] will come from east and west and will sit down [to feast at the table, and enjoy God's promises] with Abraham, Isaac, and Jacob in the kingdom of heaven [because they accepted Me as Savior]" (Matthew 8:11 AMP).*

But how is it then, if this is so, that we sit down with Abraham, Isaac and Jacob in the kingdom of heaven? Their testimony lives here and now. The effect of their faith is still alive and active now. How? It speaks to us from the grave. We sit at their table of obedience to the Lord and as recipients of the blessing and promise in Jesus Christ just as they do. They knew Him. They behold Him now. For those who follow the outward appearance of religious tradition or rites, we must remember that those things are outward signs like circumcision which should be considered nothing more than a sign of inward obedience and faith in Jesus (not Peter or any other saint...which is what counts [Romans 4:3; Galatians 3:6]). So, the answer to question "How do we sit down with them?" is quite simple. If you have ever prayed the Lord's prayer from Matthew 6:9-11, you must realize the connection here is quite fascinating. *"Thy kingdom come, thy will be done, on earth as it is in heaven."* We sit at the table of the New Covenant in His blood and partake of the body of His suffering and the promises of salvation and new life and the power of His resurrection from the dead (John 10:10; Romans 1:4; 2 Corinthians 5:17; Philippians 3:10).

On the album cover, Abraham, Isaac and Jacob stand before the great throne on which our Lord and Savior Jesus Christ sits-revealing his *completed work* (Hebrews 1:3 AMP). The promise made to them was forward looking to Christ (2 Samuel 7:19; 1 Peter 2:9) and we look back at the cross, living today in the shadow of all it represents (Isaiah 53) and the power of the resurrection (Philippians 3:10) over our enemy Satan (Luke 10:19; 1 John 4:4) who desires to destroy everything God holds dear (John 10:10b; 1 Peter 5:8).

Below is an outline of verses for your encouragement as you listen to the final album: *The End of the Age: Book Five.*

The Trumpet Sounds

♫ **Pause and listen to** *End of the Age: Book Five, "The Trumpet Sounds."* ♫

The sun (Israel, the chosen nation that rejected the Messiah [Matthew 24:30]) does not give its light. The moon (the lesser light of the Gentile nations is engaged in war [Joel 2:31; Acts 2:20]); neither will they provide light of salvation (Gospel of John chapter 1; Mark 13:24; Acts 2:20; Revelation 8:12). The Son of Man will come with thousands of saints (clouds of witnesses [Hebrews 12:1-2; Jude 1:14-15]) in power and great glory with the sound of a trumpet blast. The King (Matthew 25; Jeremiah 23:5; 30:9 AMP) will focus on *justice* and *righteousness* (Isaiah 28:16-18) in the land. Jesus will be with them and in them that follow Him (Matthew 10:22; John 17:23 AMP; Colossians 3:16; 1 Peter 3:15; Philippians 3:20). Kingdom reign is revealed and announced in Revelation 10 and Revelation 11:15 with a small scroll and a trumpet. Activity in heaven is revealed around the throne as 24 elders cast their crowns: Revelation 4:4; 4:10; 5:5; 5:8; 7:11; 11:16; 19:4. The Messiah's reign in the earth through the saints begins according to Proverbs 13:9;

Daniel 7:22; 12:3; Matthew 13:43; and Revelation 20:4-6. I know it sounds a little bit ridiculous to some. Farfetched if you will. But the promise of a savior began in Genesis 3:15 if you remember. The promise of kingdom reign and blessing in the "gates of the nations" began in the life of Abraham as previously discussed. All "kingdom of heaven" prophecy in between, the beginning and the end, just fills in the details. The Harvest of those promises is the End of the Age (Matthew 13:39 AMP).

Eyes of the Lord

♫ Pause and listen to *End of the Age: Book Five, "Eyes of the Lord."* ♫

There are several references to the "eyes of the Lord" in scripture. Basically, God sees and knows everything of everyone. He seeks for someone, like David, whose heart is completely devoted to Him and longs for righteousness and justice in the earth. This doesn't mean that the person in question is perfect; the great heroes of the Bible were not. It does mean, however, that this person would acknowledge his own weakness and depend on the grace of God (Psalm 51). It also means that he would not trust in the words of men and lean on God for his understanding (Proverbs 3:5-6). Scriptures for your perusal related to the "eyes of the Lord" include Genesis 6:8; 2 Chronicles 16:9; Psalm 10:1; Psalm 34:15; Proverbs 5:21; Proverbs 15:3; Proverbs 22:12; Zechariah 3:9; 4:10 and 1 Peter 3:12.

Shield of My Heart

♫ Pause and listen to *End of the Age: Book Five, "Shield of My Heart."* ♫

Shield of my Heart is based on Psalm 28. I have had a lot of "advice" my whole life from well-meaning religious people, particularly family. Some of them had seminary degrees and would, at family gatherings, always reminisce about the fact that they had learned Greek or Hebrew in seminary (*knowledge puffs up—1 Corinthians 8:1*). I did have one uncle, though, that was different. He was very humble and kind. When he would preach, he seemed to always be able to turn a phrase and add the following words at the end of his sermon, *"Then came Jesus,"* and present our Savior as the miracle worker He is, introducing Him into the room as the heart mender He desires to be in the given situation. He would invite Jesus into the room to minister life and healing to those present. My father was one of those who he ministered to years ago. *Then came Jesus.* My father was getting worse. *Then came Jesus.* My father's health began to improve. He survived the crash, and third degree burns over much of his body. *Then came Jesus.* This is my desire: that you would listen and meet Him in your prayer closet, experiencing those words: *then came Jesus.*

I have been misled at times by my own ambition to "know" and my misunderstandings of scripture (Proverbs 3:5-6), at times speaking out of season. Most recently I have learned to just keep quiet, sitting at Jesus' feet and listening (1 Peter 5:6). Many times, over the last two decades I have been awoken in the middle of the night to be reminded of scriptures that I had heard or read long ago during my youth (Psalm 63:6). Most recently I have become impatient with some things I see in organized religion because I do not sense much "salt" or "light" beyond the walls of the building. There are some exceptions of course. There are those who minister to the homeless, the orphans, the widows, the sick, those in prison. Those are the ones who practice *True Religion* and seek righteousness and justice in the earth. Let him have ears to hear, hear.

True Religion

♫ Pause and listen to *End of the Age: Book Five, "True Religion."* ♫

This song, referenced at the end of the previous paragraph, is based on James 1:27. The Amplified Bible includes the phrase, *"keeping oneself from becoming contaminated by the secular world."* This doesn't mean, as my pastor said, excluding and removing yourself from the secular world completely, as some do, but actively engaging the world as salt and light. This is my message: engage the world with *True Religion,* as salt and light, with righteousness and justice, preserving society and dispelling darkness. Do not forget the One who formed us as we read about Nebuchadnezzar in Daniel chapter four.

To preserve society, we must stand and speak the Word. We must stand against those that seek glory and honor from people (1 Thessalonians 2:6).

Trust the Path

♫ Pause and listen to *End of the Age: Book Five, "Trust the Path."* ♫

This song may be one of my favorites. It describes an aspect of my testimony that relates to a Bible lesson that is sometimes hard to learn: Being still and listening. Quiet your mind and heart in order to listen for God to speak to you. According to Psalms, God's law and precepts are perfect, restoring the soul (Psalm 19:7); they are a lamp unto our feet, a light unto our path (Psalm 119:105). We must know God's word first intimately. Then know Him. Jesus is the Word made Flesh. Know Jesus. Know the Word. Sit at His feet and listen for the Word to be spoken in a whisper. *Trust the Path* specifically refers to a few popular memory verses:

"Trust in and rely confidently on the Lord with all your heart And do not rely on your own insight or understanding. In all your ways know and acknowledge and recognize Him, and He will make your paths straight and smooth [removing obstacles that block your way]" (Proverbs 3:5-6 AMP).

"Whether you turn to the right or to the left, your ears will hear a voice behind you, saying, 'This is the way; walk in it'" (Isaiah 30:21 AMP).

"But the Helper (Comforter, Advocate, Intercessor-Counselor, Strengthener, Standby), the Holy Spirit, whom the Father will send in My name [in my place, to represent Me and act on My behalf], He will teach you all things. And He will help you remember everything that I have told you" (John 14:26 AMP).

The Shepherd's Call

♫ Pause and listen to *End of the Age: Book Five, "The Shepherd's Call."* ♫

The Shepherd's Call is based on Jeremiah 3:15, Matthew 25:31-35 and John 10:1-3. Jesus calls His servants to the field to gather and turn the flock towards the stable and gather them in. The goats, those who are rebellious and have refused the Word and Gift of God (John 3:16-19), will be turned aside and given a place of dishonor. Their works will be burned up (see *The Furnace Awaits* below), but many will be saved as by fire, the Word of God (Jeremiah 23:29; 1 Corinthians 3:15).

The Sword and the New Song

♫ Pause and listen to *End of the Age: Book Five, "The Sword and the New Song."* ♫

The Sword and the New Song is based primarily on Psalm 149. There are other scriptures that also refer to "a new song" which include Psalm 33:3; 40:3; 96:1; 98:1; 144:9; 149:1: and Revelation 5:9 along with Revelation 14:3. The Sword is the Sword of the Spirit, the Word of God, and the sword of Psalm 149:6.

The Furnace Awaits

♫ Pause and listen to *End of the Age: Book Five, "The Furnace Awaits."* ♫

The knowledge of God and his Word will cover the earth; that is the promise (Habakkuk 2:14). Blessings for those that believe and suffering for those who reject it. Consider Matthew 13:42-50.

The Scarlet Veil

♫ Pause and listen to *End of the Age: Book Five, "The Scarlet Veil."* ♫

I believe there are True Believers and followers of Jesus within the great Harlot and politically oriented church mentioned in Revelation 18. She sits, geographically, between seven hills. It should be mentioned that any rites or traditions regarding the "remembrance" of Christ and declaration of His death till He is revealed in all His glory are just that: acts of remembrance as we seek to follow Him in all meekness and piety. It should also me mentioned, for the sake of clarity of Biblical and Church doctrine, that the Apostle Peter was never the first "Pope." Peter was not called the "rock." When Jesus speaks to Peter in Matthew 16:18, the reference to "rock" refers to the *revelation* that Jesus was the Christ, the Messiah, the Anointed One. We do not follow Peter. We confess Peter's confession: Jesus was and is the Messiah and Savior. We follow Jesus. We worship Jesus. We honor Jesus. For it was the Father's delight to put everything under His feet (1 Corinthians 15:27; Ephesians 1:22). He is our High Priest (Hebrews 4:14). Be careful, also, of how you pray (Matthew 6:5-7).

Return of the King

♫ Pause and listen to *End of the Age: Book Five, "Return of the King."* ♫

Whether this song is about the rule of one king or more (2 Timothy 2:12; 1 Corinthians 6:3; 1 Peter 2:9 [king-priests]; Matthew 25:34-40; Obadiah 1:21 ASV [saviours—delegated *servants* or *angels*]; Jeremiah 23:15; 30:9; Amos 9:11; Luke 1:69; Revelation 11:15), is not for me to say. It is for you to discern through prayer and knowledge of God's Word. One thing is for certain; the leadership will delegate and give commands to the saints to gather his chosen leaders for the harvest at the end of the age. The "end of the age" is not a literal end of all things, rather it is the beginning of the age of renewal spoken of by Jesus (Matthew 19:28)

Important note regarding Bible headings

The headings in our Bibles, except for most all of those in the Psalms of David, are not inspired. I was prompted by the Holy Spirit to investigate this as I was writing this book and found several blogs and authors that confirmed my suspicion. As you consider these passages, be sure to skip over the headings in the New Testament and read only the text, which is inspired. For example, my Bible includes the following headings in Matthew 24: *Signs of Christ's Return* and *The Glorious Return.* Those headings were placed there by Bible editors and translators. It is more appropriate, in my most humble opinion, to interpret these passages as parallel passages for the time of restoration and renewal mentioned by Jesus and during which the *Son of Man* sits on his glorious (Isaiah 61; Matthew 19:28; Colossians 3:11; Acts 3:21).

The Angel's Scroll

♫ **Pause and listen to** *End of the Age: Book Five, "The Angel's Scroll."* ♫

A small scroll reveals the mystery hidden for ages by God to be revealed in the last days. It is the inheritance (Isaiah 65:9) of the saints (Matthew 25:34; Ephesians 5:5; Proverbs 25:2; Revelation 10:7). Its revealing is for the blessing and healing of the nations (Genesis 22:17-18; Revelation 22:2). If you haven't read Daniel 4 yet, it is worth mentioning that kings and nations that do not humble themselves and walk humbly before God will be judged severely just as king Nebuchadnezzar. Only when he recognized God as sovereign and repented of his pride and vanity did God restore his sanity and heal him.

The Final Dawn

♫ **Pause and listen to** *End of the Age: Book Five, "The Final Dawn."* ♫

Jesus referred to a time of renewal in the earth, which, as I understand now, would refer to the millennial reign in which the saints possess the kingdoms (Daniel 7:18-22; Matthew 19:28; Isaiah 61). In Matthew 19:28 Jesus does not refer to Himself sitting on His glorious throne (in heaven), but to someone else—someone who overcomes and shares His throne with Him (Psalm 2:9; Revelation 2:17-27; Revelation 3:12; Revelation 3:21; Revelation 12:5; Revelation 19:15; Revelation 21:7), just as we read in Matthew 25:34-40).

What is our purpose during this time and always? To lift up and glorify God's Son, Jesus Christ, in every corner of the earth so that He may draw all men to Himself so that they may be reconciled, brought near, to God; to possess the gates of the enemy; to judge justly; to lift the standard; to be salt and light; to protect those who cannot speak for themselves; to free those imprisoned in human trafficking.... You get the idea.

The Feast of the Kingdom

♫ Pause and listen to *End of the Age: Book Five, "Feast of the Kingdom."* ♫

Based primarily on Matthew 8:11 (mentioned previously), *The Feast of the Kingdom* speaks to the fact that all the promises of God are *yes and amen* in Jesus Christ (2 Corinthians 1:20 AMP). Additional references might include the power of the Resurrection of Christ (1 Corinthians 15) and remembering it at His table (Matthew 8:11; 1 Corinthians 11:23-26). As we reflect on this and the verse in Matthew 8:11, we sit down at a banquet table of promises that are not kept from us in any way. Rather, the Father, if we are *in* His Son and He is in us, gives us generously and bountifully all His blessings and promises. For the Father delights in giving us the kingdom (Luke 12:32). One of the most coveted promises is peace: peace with God and men (Romans 12:18).

"Peace I leave with you; My [perfect] peace I give to you; not as the world gives do I give to you. Do not let your heart be troubled, nor let it be afraid. [Let my perfect peace calm you in every circumstance and give your courage and strength for every challenge]" (John 14:27 AMP).

Kadosh, Kadosh, Kadosh (Holy, Holy, Holy)

♫ Pause and listen to *End of the Age: Book Five, "Kadosh, Kadosh, Kadosh."* ♫

The Testimony of Jesus, and Book Five, both end with the same exclamation point: Jesus is Holy, Holy, Holy. He is the Alpha and Omega. He is the beginning and the end...Only in Him do we find living, eternal water to satisfy our hungry soul (John 4:13-14; Revelation 21:6). In Him all things consist, were made and are sustained (Colossians 1:16AMP). In Him we live and move and exist (Acts 17:11).

Closing Remarks

Many counselors (Proverbs 11:14) are required to complete what I believe God would have us do. What I have prepared for you is my investigation and testimony that has taken me on a very demanding journey lasting almost 25 years. It is my legacy gift to you. I will leave you with one quote from a book that my mother gave to me years ago that is even more poignant today than when it was written:

> *"...the deliberate application of the techniques of theater to politics, religion, education, literature, commerce, warfare, crime, everything, has converted them into branches of show business, where the overriding objective is getting and satisfying an audience."*

Neil Gabler, Life the Movie: How Entertainment Conquered Reality

Audience. Who is your audience? Is Jesus your audience. Are you His disciple? Do you let Him teach you? Are you His audience of one? Do you renew your mind with His word so you can understand what His will is (Romans 12:1-2)? Are you strengthened in your inner being (Ephesians 3:16)?

I referred to author Neil Gabler a moment ago. He cites Daniel Boorstin who said we are shifting from "ideal-thinking" (values and aspirations) to "image-thinking" (surface, representation and appearance). Gabler refers to a "post-reality culture," where illusions become so vivid and persuasive that they supplant actual lived experience. Those thoughts consider serious contemplation as we try to *reframe* our lives through the lens of God's Word. *Reframing* ideas and conforming, renewing our mind with the Word of God is no easy task these days. If anything, I have said here has spoken to you, underline it. Take notes. Discuss it in a small group. Make it a matter of prayer and transformation. If it is a scripture that has taken hold of your heart, meditate on the scriptures. Renew your mind...and your confession (what you say).

The Fatherless and Unborn

♫ Pause and listen to *End of the Age: Book Two, "In Need of a Father."* ♫

As I was writing this last page, an article came across my desk published by AMAC magazine. The author and alumna of Hillsdale College, Sarah Katherine, presented a few strong arguments for the decline of American society including the following. First, 63 million children have been aborted since *Roe V. Wade*, including 24.5 million millennials and 26 million members of Gen Z, nearly a third of both generations. Proponents of abortion, she points out, promote abortion due to rape, incest and life-threatening pregnancies to justify the practice. But all those combined reasons count for less than 5 percent of the reasons for abortion. This means that all the rest were "elected procedures." Second, and quite troubling, is the steady increase in fatherless children since 1960. She explains that for decades government programs have reinforced these pressures by incentivizing fatherlessness due to the way welfare is designed. In 1960, 11 percent of kids were living in homes without fathers (of course, "fatherhood" has evolved and changed over the years regarding types of fathers. I'm not going to discuss that now). By 2020, that figure had doubled. In 2023, an estimated 55.4 percent of black kids were living in a single-parent home. How are we to address this? First, pause and reflect on what scripture says about fathers and their role from the very beginning. The power of a father to bless and direct his family is underestimated.

The Father's Blessing

In the book of Genesis and throughout the Bible we read of God-fearing men spiritually and verbally blessing and teaching their children (Genesis 18:19); Deuteronomy 4:10) in the name of God and teaching them by example, praying for them, with them and teaching them to obey God. The leaders spoke to the people (Joshua 1:8) and the people spoke to their children (Proverbs 22:6; Psalm 34:11; Colossians 3:21). In Genesis we see that the blessing from the father carried great weight and power and was coveted by the children of Isaac, Jacob and Esau. Today, each child goes his own way. Yet, there is hope:

"He will turn the hearts of the fathers to their children, and the hearts of the children to their fathers [a reconciliation produced by repentance], so that I will not come and strike the land with a curse [of complete destruction]" (Malachi 4:6 AMP).

"Behold, children are a heritage and gift from the LORD, The fruit of the womb a reward. Like arrows in the hand of a warrior, so are the children of one's youth. How blessed [happy and fortunate] is the man whose quiver is filled with

them; They will not be ashamed When they speak with their enemies [in gatherings] at the [city] gate" (Psalm 127:3-5).

"but whoever cause one of these little ones who believe in Me to stumble and sin [by leading him away from My teaching], it would be better for him to have a heavy millstone [as large as one turned by a donkey] hung around his neck and to be drowned in the depth of the sea" (Matthew 18:6 AMP).

Men, pray with and for your family. Unplug from the entertainment world regularly and sit at Jesus feet. Have Bible studies in your home. Pray with your children. Love God and your neighbors in word an deed. Study God's Word with your children. Take your children into the community to share and serve. Go with your church into the prisons and share the Gospel of John. Donate to organizations sending Bibles into the 10-40 window. Be salt. Be light. Shine bright. Put on the armor of Ephesians 6. Kneel. Sit. Be taught. Then go. Fight. Stand (Psalm 110:3).

The End of the Matter

"When all has been heard, the end of the matter is: fear God [worship Him with awe-filled reverence, knowing that He is almighty God] and keep His commandments, for his applies to every person" (Ecclesiastes 12:13 AMP).

I know nothing of Christ's return. I do know that He is to be revealed in and through the Church during Harvest at the *end of the age* in such a way that has never been seen before and that the saints will overcome the world with justice and righteousness. It will certainly continue to be a time of trouble for a time until the kingdom gives birth (*birth pains*) to the kingdom age of renewal and regeneration when the kingdoms stand silent before the cross.

So, be strong and courageous (Joshua 1:8). Be wise and Spirit-led (Romans 8:14) like the Apostle Paul. Sing like David (Ephesians 5:19). Be strong like Sampson (but don't fall into the trap he did and lose your strength). Remember the last prayer of Sampson? He prayed to God and asked for strength to carry away the doors to the gates of the city (Judges 16:2-4). We may be weak. But He is strong in us. Pray for that strength. It is time to collapse the gates of the wicked city and rebuild the city of God, the city of living stones, the New Jerusalem. From here we will build it up. For those who believe the truth, it is revealed from above and comes down—for all truth comes down and is revealed from heaven.

God wants us to choose life so that we may be blessed. The first scripture that speaks to this was spoken to Israel. But we must remember that all the promises of God are *yes and amen* in Christ and that there is no difference between Jew and non-Jew at the foot of the cross (Deuteronomy 30; Romans 3:22; 4:16; 10:12; 15:9).

Revisiting the Cloud of Witnesses Past and Present

What is the meaning of Jesus coming in the *clouds?* Is it not because He lives and dwells within us now? Is it not that we have put our faith in Him just as the cloud of witnesses that has gone before (Romans 5:2; Hebrews 11:1-12:2; 2 Corinthians 4:6; Colossians 1:27)? Does it mean that we will set aside our division created by religious traditions and unite as one as He and the Father are one as He prayed in John 17:23 AMP so that the world might believe? Yes. For we have this glory in jars of clay, our bodies, so that the glory may be of God (2 Corinthians 4:7).

Come to the Table of the Living Witnesses Past and Present

We call the nations to come to the covenant wedding table. For in Him we live and move and exist (Matthew 8:11; 22; Matthew 22:32; Mark 12:25-27; Mark 14:22-23; Act 17:28; 1 Corinthians 11:23-26 AMP).

If they reject Him, then God rejects them as well (John 3:16-19 AMP).

May God bless all of you and strengthen you in this difficult time of trouble.

Here are some lyrics from a song that comes to mind that was not published in any of my albums:

"God calls to the volunteers and the watchmen;
He calls the elect and the redeemed:
'Come and stand under the mountain,
The time has come to make peace.
Trumpet with your voice,
Trumpet with the strings,
Trumpet with the tambourine.

Gather the elect around David's throne,
And speak the mysteries that must be known.'"

My brothers and sisters stand in the gates of the city, in the presence of judges and kings. Lift the standard. Spread the news. Take counsel (Proverbs 15:22). Speak with the breath of Jesus, with the fire of His Word, Sword and Light. Honor the two greatest commandments that Jesus taught (Matthew 22:37-39). Honor the testimony of saints and martyrs. Worship no man. For our God is not the God of the dead, but of the living (Matthew 22:32). 'Your kingdom come, your will be done on earth as it is in heaven' (Matthew 6:10 AMP).

Sincerely,
Sanctus Matthews

P. S. So now, go and publish on your own and in every language you can: 1) your testimony along with 2) John 3:16-18; Matthew 24:22; Mark 8:11 and 3) the works of the wicked.